TO MEET THE REAL DRAGON

TO MEET THE REAL DRAGON

Seeking The Truth In A World Of Chaos

Gudo Wafu Nishijima
Jeffrey Alan Bailey

Wind-bell Publications

© 1984 in Japan by Wind-bell Publications, Ltd.

Published by Wind-bell Publications, Ltd.
28-3 Matsuba-cho, Tokorozawa, Saitama, Japan

Distributors:

Japan: JAPAN PUBLICATIONS TRADING CO., LTD.
1-2-1 Sarugaku-cho, Chiyoda-ku, Tokyo 101, Japan

United States: J.P. TRADING, INC.
300 Industrial Way, Brisbane, California 94005

First edition: April, 1984

ISBN 0-87040-594-2

Printed in Japan

CONTENTS

PREFACE

My name is Nishijima. I am a Buddhist priest. I became a priest rather late in my life, and since it took me so long to find my true calling, I took the name Gudo at the time of my ordination. Gu means straight or stupid. Do means Truth or Way. Even a stupid man can find the Truth.

So I am rather slow and stupid, but I have lived about sixty years now, and during more than forty of those years, I have practiced the Buddhist life and studied Buddhist philosophy. Slowly and surely I have walked my straight and stupid path. Slowly and surely I have learned the meaning of this life. I have learned how to live.

For myself then, I am content. But for my companions on this earth, I feel much concern. We have entered a time of great confusion and danger. The conflicts between us have become sharp and menacing. The possibility of nuclear war is real. I am very concerned.

At the same time I am hopeful. For as the conflicts between us have sharpened, they have, at the same time, been clarified. The choices confronting us appear as black and white. We see East and West, left and right, liberalism and conservatism, idealism and materialism. We can see two sides clearly now. So we are living in a situation of heightened tension—a dangerous situation, but also a hopeful situation. For when we can see two sides clearly, the middle ground also becomes visible. Buddhism occupies this middle ground. It is the Middle Way. But the Middle Way is not a compromise. It is a clear choice, a clear alternative. To walk in the Middle Way is to reject the extremes and enter the real world.

Buddhist theory points the way to that world. I hope this book can point the way clearly and directly. We need clear directions in these confusing times. But who will follow the directions? Who will abandon the security of their prejudices and one-sided views of reality? Where, in this world of confusion and conflict, are there people who are ready to step into the real world?

I look to America. It is a splendid land, a wide and diverse land. It was born on a vast continent and produced through the trials and effort, the blood and sweat of pioneers. And it retains the spirit of those pioneers: optimism, practicality, and a willingness to experiment, to try new things. Most civilizations are bound by the accumulated weight of tradition, but America is still young, still growing and evolving.

A civilization in its youth, like a young person, must experience the pains of youth: the pain of confusion, the pain of maturing, the pain of finding direction and meaning. Thus far in its history, America seems to have followed the principle of trial and error in its efforts to find its way. Trial and error is an excellent and useful tool, but at some point, the experiences of life must be seen as a pattern; some theory or principle must evolve to guide the civilization in its maturity.

I feel that America is looking for direction; searching for a unifying philosophy: a fundamental point of view on which to base its actions, its life. But how can a civilization as wide and diverse as America ever find a unifying philosophy? What single principle could accomodate the hopes and desires, the beliefs and habits of a nation like the United States?

I think Buddhism could accomplish that task. I think Buddhism could be the unifying philosophy America is seeking. I think so because Buddhism is a philosophy which welcomes all points of view, studies them critically, and then steps beyond them into reality—into the real world. If America could find Buddhism— if it could study Buddhism, absorb Buddhism, and transform Buddhism according to its own character; then it would have its needed theory; it would have the unifying philosophy it needs to harness its energy, synthesize its diversity, and grow into a truly great civilization. This is the hope I have for America. This is the hope I have for us all.

If this hope is to be realized, Buddhism and America must meet. They must be introduced. A conversation must be begun and a long, long dialogue must ensue. However, if this communication is to be successful, both sides must speak the same language. We are living in the modern world. The modern world is an intellectual world, a world of theory and logic. Buddhism has a very profound and embracing logic, a theoretical system which can be precisely translated into concepts familiar to this world. I discovered this theoretical system in a book called the *Shōbōgenzō*. It was written over 700 years ago by a Japanese Zen master, Master Dogen. I believe that the *Shōbōgenzō* could be the basis for a dialogue between the Western world and Buddhism. I would like to introduce the *Shōbōgenzō* to America. I would like to begin the conversation between America and Buddhism—at once!

ABOUT THIS BOOK

The idea of a dialogue is important to me. A few years ago I resolved to begin a dialogue with the West. At that time I was giving lectures on Buddhism and the *Shōbōgenzō* to my Japanese students every week. I decided to begin lectures in English once a month to see if there was interest in such matters among foreigners living in Tokyo. This was not an easy task for me. My English speaking ability was not good. But I have always felt that if we want to do something we must begin. We must start from where we are and do our best. And so I did. Among the foreigners who came to one of my lectures, out of curiosity or an interest in Zen, a few came back a second and a third time and eventually became regular members. I felt this was encouraging and so decided to have the seminar in English every week just prior to the Japanese lecture. Between the lectures we all practiced zazen for an hour. It was a nice beginning.

Then I began to search for a means of presenting the philosophy of the *Shōbōgenzō* to a wider audience. As a step in that direction, I started work on a book I had been envisioning for some time. It was in the form of a dialogue between a Westerner and a Buddhist master. I called it, "Buddhism: Questions and Answers." But when I showed the rough draft of my book to some of my foreign friends, they were only mildly encouraging. They said that my primitive English and rather simple way of explaining Buddhist concepts would not be well received in the West, where sophistication and complexity are often seen as the mark of serious thought and scholarship. Their doubts undermined my own confidence; I began to wonder if the gap between the American public and this simple Japanese man was really too wide to be bridged.

Then one day, Mr. Bailey, a young American from the English seminar, came to visit me in my office. I told him of my problem. I asked him if the Pacific was too wide. Mr. Bailey felt that somehow the great ocean could be crossed. He offered his help. So I had found a partner. From that time on, Mr. Bailey and I met every week to discuss Buddhism and the writing of a book about the *Shōbōgenzō*. We decided to abandon the original form of my draft and instead to use the weekly seminars as the framework for the book. The questions and answers in the original draft became themes in my continuing lectures. Mr. Bailey worked to edit those lectures and to find the connecting thread

PREFACE

of ideas which would give the final work a sense of logic and continuity. During our private discussions, he checked and re-checked his understanding of what I was trying to say. Thus, the dialogue I had envisioned as a book became a real dialogue between Mr. Bailey and myself.

This book is the first product of that dialogue. Since it is a first effort, the reader should not expect a work of finished perfection, but a work in progress—a work which at times reveals the limitations of the authors and the very real limitations of language itself. In spite of these shortcomings, I am proud of this book. I think it points the way to a new world—to a world which is always here, but which we seldom see. It is a splendid world, a fine place in which to live. This world is your birthright as a human being. I invite you to claim your birthright. I invite you to share fully in the splendid reality which is this world: the real world, here and now.

Gudo Wafu Nishijima

SOME EXPLANATION

The first draft of this book was completed over two years ago, in the fall of 1980. Then, flushed with pride and excitement, Reverend Nishijima and I presented it to one of the leading publishers here in Tokyo. A few months later we received their politely worded, but clearly negative verdict. The book offered nothing startlingly new in the field of Buddhist or Zen studies. The market was already over-crowded with "Introductions to Zen." Publishing another would not be economically sound.

We were disappointed, but not discouraged. We began to look for other ways of publishing the book and, at the same time, sought ways of improving it. Several of Reverend Nishijima's students and acquaintances read the manuscript and offered their comments and criticism. One of those students, a British engineer named Michael Luetchford, was concerned that my own role in writing the book had not been fully explained. Readers would naturally be curious, he felt, about who I was, what kind of background I had had, and just how much of my own thought and experience had found its way into the pages of the book.

I answered that it was really impossible for me to judge the extent of my influence on the content of the book. I had done my best to preserve the original feeling of Reverend Nishijima's lectures—to express his ideas directly and simply, as he himself did. I had tried to convey the spirit of the man as well as the content of his thought, and to this end, I had sought to submerge my own thoughts and sensibilities as much as possible. My role had been, essentially, that of a ghost writer.

This being so, I felt that it was better for me to remain as inconspicuous as possible. Interjecting my own personality, even in an introduction, would only confuse and distract the reader. As Reverend Nishijima might say: "It is the duty of ghosts to remain invisible."

Mr. Luetchford did not press me on this issue, but I could see that he was not convinced. Rationally, I felt that my position was sound, but, deep down, I knew that it was not entirely honest. The truth was that I was simply more comfortable being invisible. I was more than a little apprehensive about having my work scrutinized by experts, by scholars who knew much more about Buddhism and philosophy than I. At the same time I enjoyed the faint aura of mystery that my anonymity provided.

Having seen through my intellectual rationale for remaining invisible, I felt compelled to do something about it. I wrote a series of autobiographical sketches, each one more self-consciously "honest and revealing" than the one before. In spite of my efforts, something did not seem to ring true. I began to wonder if the self I was revealing was real or imaginary, fact or fiction. At that point, I threw away my notes and concluded that my original resolve to remain anonymous had been correct after all. But the feeling that I should write something persisted, and as time went by, I explored various other approaches to the problem.

Then, in the fall of 1982, I began giving English lessons to Reverend Nishijima on a daily basis. Although his reading comprehension was fairly good, he was still struggling to come to terms with the spoken language; at his age, that is quite an undertaking.

SOME EXPLANATION

For teaching material, I decided to use *The Tao of Physics*, by Fritjof Capra. Reverend Nishijima had already read and enjoyed the book, and I felt that the author had done a good job of explaining a difficult subject in plain language—a problem which Reverend Nishijima faces constantly in his lectures.

One morning, an issue arose to which Reverend Nishijima reacted quite strongly. We talked about it for some time, and I took a few notes, but, as is often the case, the full significance of his words did not strike me until some time later. Then, as bits and pieces of our conversation came back to mind, a variety of thoughts and memories seemed to sort themselves out in my consciousness. I had a feeling of learning something—a rather nice feeling. The next morning I told Reverend Nishijima about my experience, and his comments helped me to see things more clearly and objectively than before. Later, I was thinking about the entire chain of thoughts and events surrounding my little moment of insight, and it occurred to me that, if I could reconstruct that chain on paper, it might prove to be as interesting and revealing as anything else I might write to explain myself, my role in writing this book, or my relationship with Reverend Nishijima. At least it was worth a try.

On the morning in question, we were reading a few paragraphs from the first chapter of *The Tao of Physics*. Mr. Capra had just completed a brief overview of the historical development of scientific and philosophical thought and had begun to talk about what he saw as one outcome of that development: the tendency of modern man to see himself and the world in parts or fragments. As an example of the "inner fragmentation of man," he spoke of the fact that most people are aware of themselves as "isolated egos existing 'inside' their bodies." "The mind has (thus) been separated from the body and given the futile task of controlling it."

He then went on to talk about the analogous tendency to see the external world in bits and pieces, rather than as an organic whole. In this view, nature becomes a mere collection of exploitable parts; human society is broken down into abstract entities: nations, races, religious and political groups, and so on; and the entire fabric of life is shredded into small pieces.

"The belief," he concludes, "that all these fragments—in ourselves, in our environment and in our society—are really separate can be seen as the essential reason for the present series of social, ecological and cultural crises. It has alienated us from nature and from our fellow human beings. It has brought a grossly unjust distribution of natural resources creating economic and political disorder; an ever rising wave of violence, both spontaneous and institutionalized, and an ugly, polluted environment in which life has often become physically and mentally unhealthy."

It was, all in all, a rather sweeping indictment, but one which appeared fairly familiar and reasonable to me. Reverend Nishijima's reaction was quite to the contrary, however.

"He is wrong!" he said.

Somewhat startled, I asked him why.

"The fundamental problem of modern man is not his tendency to intellectualize."

"But," I protested, "you have talked about this problem over and over again in your lectures. One whole chapter of our book is devoted to this idea."

"Yes," he said, "our tendency to see the world in parts and to believe that those divisions really exist is an important problem. It contributes to and perhaps underlies much of our confusion, much of the chaotic feeling in our lives. But—it is not the fundamental problem. It is not the real problem in our human societies today."

SOME EXPLANATION

"So what is the 'real problem.'"

"The real problem is that people today have lost the foundation
of their lives. They have lost the basis on which to construct
their systems of belief. In short, they have lost their gods."

"Their gods?"

"Yes, their gods. Throughout history and especially since the
time of the Renaissance in Europe, materialistic theories and
philosophies have mounted successive attacks on mankind's
belief in the gods of traditional religions. Empiricist philosophy, Marxism, Darwinism and Freudianism—scientific theories
of all kinds—have steadily undermined our ability to believe
in a spiritual god: a being outside the material universe, yet
somehow creating and controlling it.

"At the same time, our faith in the omniscient and ultimately
benevolent character of science was shattered forever by the
dawn of the nuclear age. Few of us who remember Hiroshima and
Nagasaki can ever have absolute confidence in scientific progress or in the ability of man to control the forces he has
unleashed. The god of natural science has been shown to be a
fickle god—an unworthy object of our belief.

"So, yes, I believe we have lost our gods. And having lost our
gods, we have lost the center of our life. We have lost the
foundation we need to sit calmly amidst the confusion that is
life itself. And so we are looking. We are searching for a new
foundation, a new Truth. This is our situation in the modern
world, and this is our fundamental problem."

I had heard the same theme expressed in various ways many times
in the course of my association with Reverend Nishijima. Perhaps because of that familiarity, his words did not make a
particularly strong impression on me at the time. We concluded
our lesson a few minutes later, and I went off to earn my
living teaching English to Japanese students and businessmen.

TO MEET THE REAL DRAGON

That evening I had some free time so I decided to take a walk in the quiet neighborhood near my apartment. As I walked, some snatches of the morning's discussion played through my mind, and I began to make some connections between Reverend Nishijima's words and my own experience.

I began to think of my early attraction to and ultimate disillusionment with the two gods Reverend Nishijima had spoken of. I remembered my hesitant, sometimes painful, and always confused relationship with the "traditional religion" of my parents'. I remembered my efforts to be "good" according to the dictates of that religion, my efforts to find out just what it meant to pray, and my efforts to understand to whom or to what I was praying. And I remembered the overriding feelings which those sincere efforts produced in the end: feelings of anger, frustration, and resentment.

My memories of the second god, the god of science, were generally more positive, especially in the early stages. I was nicknamed "nature boy" by one of my science teachers, a man I loved and admired. He taught me the excitement of observing the world—of finding names, concepts, and explanations for what I observed. Through the personal tragedy of his own life, he also taught me another important lesson: that knowledge of science is not knowledge of life—that learning how to live is something entirely different, something entirely removed from the learning of facts, figures, and scientific theories.

When I had seen this fact clearly, it somehow took the joy out of my study of science. I became alternately cynical about the "advances" of science and morose about my own inferior intellect, about the hopelessness of my ever really understanding anything.

Perhaps these experiences of my youth were typical of many of my generation. Perhaps they represented my own personal loss of the gods of religion and science; and perhaps, as Reverend Nishijima suggested, it was that loss which prompted my search for, and my openness to, other options, other explanations. I remembered then the words my mother had spoken when, after dropping out of college, I joined the Peace Corps and left for India: "Well, I hope you find what you're looking for." And she had repeated the same words some six years later when I went off to "meditate" at a center for Tibetan Buddhist studies. It was, no doubt, that constant search for something, something I myself couldn't name, that had eventually brought me here to Japan and to Reverend Nishijima's lectures.

From such reveries, my thoughts turned to my present situation. What had I gained by my four years of study and practice? Had I found the foundation which Reverend Nishijima said we were looking for? Perhaps. At times it did seem that there was something different in the quality of my life. There was nothing I could point to positively—nothing very exceptional or dramatic. Just a kind of feeling: an occasional sense of calmness or serenity. Nothing great. Nothing exciting. Perhaps, I thought to myself, this was what Reverend Nishijima meant when he spoke of seeing things as they are. Perhaps I had finally begun to give up the dream of enlightenment—the dream of some dramatic change in my life, or in my understanding of life.

What was it he had said?—"We have lost the foundation we need to sit calmly amidst the confusion that is life." These words seemed to suggest that the confusion of life is not something to be feared or eliminated. Rather we need find solid ground on which to sit and watch the show. We need not yearn for any dramatic change or clear understanding. We need only the equanimity that comes from knowing that this is, in fact, the way things are.

So this is where my thinking had led. This was the little insight which had given me a moments happiness, a moments satisfaction. To many, it may not seem like much, but to me, at that time, it seemed very important indeed. The next morning I asked Reverend Nishijima what he thought of my idea.

TO MEET THE REAL DRAGON

"You are right," he said. "You have seen the point which many Buddhist scholars and priests have failed to appreciate. They think that Buddhism exists in books or in temples. For a few days or a few weeks each year they may exert themselves in severe practice, but then they have a beer and return to what they see as the rat race: the complicated situations of everyday life. They think that such complicated situations have nothing to do with Buddhism, with religion, or with the sacred in life, but this is, in fact, where true Buddhism resides. This is where the sacred exists. It is in the ordinary, confused and complicated affairs of everyday life that we can find the meaning of life, the meaning of the Truth.

"Most people want to escape from such complicated situations. They want to get rid of confusion and the humdrum concerns of daily existence. They become anxious and compound the problem, making simple confusion into vivid chaos. But if they could study true Buddhism and practice true Buddhism everyday, they would soon find that there is something splendid in the complicated affairs of that day-to-day existence. They would find that they need not get rid of confusion. They would learn instead to ride the stormy waves that form the ocean of life. Then, swimming vigorously in that sometimes stormy, sometimes calm and balmy sea, they would find the real world, as it is. They would find the Truth."

Such are the words of a Buddhist master. Reverend Nishijima is my Master, my Teacher or Sensei. When he warms up to a favorite subject, his voice becomes full and vibrant. There is a touch of urgency in his tone, and his words take on a peculiar kind of eloquence, an eloquence I have seldom heard in my life. It is, I believe, the eloquence of Truth.

Jeffrey Bailey

ACKNOWLEDGMENTS

With this trial edition, "the dragon book" has finally become a reality. The circuitous route by which we have come to this point is something of a story in itself, but the details of the story are perhaps of interest only to those who were intimately involved. Some of the participants in our little drama are listed below. Each of them contributed in some small or large way to the writing, editing, or publishing of the book. We regret that we cannot cite their contributions individually, but we would like to express our sincere appreciation to each of them for their efforts in our behalf. We hope that their involvement in our project has been or will be in some way rewarding to them. Most especially we hope that they will be inspired to seek the Truth—that the "Real Dragon" will find a place in their day-to-day lives.

Lisa Braun, Inge Brouard, Franklin Buchanan, Bill Clavell, Mike Cross, Stephen Cruise, Heather Gibb, Hideo Ida, Michael and Yoko Luetchford, Masao Ohta, Keiko Ohtsubo, Robert Phillips, Rene Rebetez, Barbara Sloan, Penelope Takahashi, Fuyumi Tamura, Alice Wand, Larry Zacchi.

WHAT IS RELIGION ?

Happy New Year! A Happy New Year to You! In Japan we feel that New Year's Day is a very special time. It is the beginning of a new life for us, a time of renewal and hope; it is a very happy day. It is our custom to place a small pine bough on the front door as a symbol of the New Year. When we see the pine bough, it reminds us of this special time and makes us feel very good.

But about 500 years ago there was a Buddhist priest, named Ikkyu, who said that the pine bough on the front gate was a marker on the way to death. That's not a very pleasant thought, is it? But isn't there some truth to his words? Each year when we look at the bough, we are reminded that we have aged one more year; we are one year closer to our death. So from this perspective perhaps New Year's Day is not such a happy time after all. What do you think? Is New Year's Day a happy time or not? Is the pine bough a symbol of life or death?

If you asked a Buddhist he might smile and say it is both, or he might say it is neither, or he might ask you to show him the difference between December 31st and January 1st. They are both 24 hours long. The sun rises in the east on December 31st, and on January 1st it does the same. Perhaps there is no difference between the two days. From a certain point of view, they appear to be the same. In fact, when we look at life in a certain way it seems that every day is the same day.

So now what do you think? Is January 1st a happy day, a sad day, or just another day like any other day? It's difficult to decide, isn't it? It all depends on how we look at the question. It depends on our point of view. I think our point of view is very important. Usually we look at life from only one standpoint. It is a kind of habit. But, as the example of New Year's Day shows, there are many ways of looking at life. We are all aware of this fact. We know that different people tend to see things differently. Some people have a positive, hopeful outlook; others always see the dark side of life. Some people are very practical, while others seem to walk around with their heads in the clouds. The differences among people are numerous and interesting. They are a natural part of life. But when we encounter viewpoints which are different from our own, we usually feel uneasy. Sometimes we laugh, sometimes we scoff, sometimes we become very angry. In every case we seem to cling to our own point of view. We try to protect ourselves from viewpoints which are alien to our own way of thinking. This is a problem for us—a rather big problem.

Of course it is not too difficult to be open-minded when it comes to a simple question like the meaning of New Year's Day. No one would fight over such an insignificant issue. But what happens when we consider more controversial subjects? Take religion for example. People generally have rather strong feelings about religion. Either they accept religion as a natural and necessary part of their lives, or they carefully avoid anything which resembles religion or religious thought. Very few people really consider the meaning of religion itself. But I think it is important to look closely at that which we call religion. I think we should ask ourselves a very fundamental question: What is religion, anyway?

This question became important to me many years ago. I was one of those people who are naturally attracted to religious ideas.

WHAT IS RELIGION?

I became interested in Buddhism when I was rather young, and I read many books about it. In some of those books, I found a very interesting debate. It seemed that some scholars doubted whether or not Buddhism was a religion. They insisted that a "true religion" must recognize the existence of a god, a supernatural realm, or a power in the universe which is beyond and apart from this material world. But Buddhism does not have such a belief. Buddhism looks no further than this place and time for its inspiration. Buddhism affirms this world. It was this affirmation of the real world that the religious scholars found troubling, and because of it many of them could not bring themselves to include Buddhism in the family of true religions. This was very surprising to me. There was something strange about a definition of religion which could not accept the possibility of a "realistic" religion. In my life Buddhism was religion itself. How could it not be a religion? But here in these books scholars were seriously debating whether Buddhism was a religion or not. So I began to wonder what "religion" was. I asked myself what all religions had in common.

Finding a common ground for all religions was not so easy. When I studied the religions of the world, I found great diversity in their beliefs and practices. In some cases those beliefs and practices appeared to be similar, but there were also many fundamental differences. There were exceptions to every rule. It seemed that every definition of religion was either too narrow and limited or too complicated to be really useful. Then one day I noticed a very simple fact. I saw that while religious beliefs and practices were very diverse, the simple existence of such beliefs and practices was something all religions had in common. At first this observation seemed too simple and obvious to be of much importance, but later I realized that it was, in fact, very useful in clarifying the fundamental nature of religion. Every religion has its philosophy, its particular understanding of life. The followers of the religion believe in that philosophy and they act according to their belief. This is, I think, the essence of religion. I think all religions have these two factors in common; that is, belief in a certain theory or philosophy and actual conduct in accord with that belief.

This simple definition of religion has rather far reaching implications. When we think of religion in this way, many of our common-sense notions about religion become untenable. Usually we think that there are religious people and irreligious people, that life divides itself neatly between the religious and the secular, the sacred and the profane. But if we use my simple definition of religion, such a division becomes irrelevant. All men have a philosophy, some understanding of the world which guides them in their day-to-day lives. They may not adhere to any formal religion or philosophy, but still they have their own very personal understanding of life and the world they live in. Some philosophers call this personal understanding of life our "world-view". It is this world-view which serves all people as the standpoint from which to decide their actions, their conduct in society. So I think religion is something much more basic and universal than most people realize. At the most fundamental level, I think that all men have a religion; that they cannot, in fact, live without a religion. What do you think?

QUESTIONS & ANSWERS

Many people claim that they don't have any religion, don't they?

Yes, many people insist that they have no religion, but I think it is only an insistence. In fact, they believe in the religion called non-religion. In their day-to-day lives their behavior is based on the belief that there is no god and nothing of spiritual value in the world. This is their philosophy, their personal view of life, and while such philosophies seem much different from those of traditional religions, their effects on the lives and behavior of the "believers" are much the same. So even though such people think they have no religion, an

objective observer can readily see they are followers of the
religion called non-religion.

*Do you recognize any distinction between religion and philos-
ophy?*

The distinction between religion and philosophy is often obscure, but I think there is a definite difference between them.
Philosophy, in its purest form, is an intellectual study of
ideas, a study of theories and principles. It is quite possible to study philosophical ideas without being touched by them.
We can analyze them, compare them, construct them into grand
systems and still not be influenced by them in any real sense.
But if we come to believe in the ideas—decisively and wholeheartedly—and to use them as a kind of standard of living,
then we have moved from the realm of pure philosophy into the
realm of religion. In the realm of religion, ideas have the
power to influence our actions in the real world. This is the
power of belief, and it is the attitude of sincere belief which
distinguishes a religion from a philosophy.

*If we accept your definition, it would seem that there must be
as many religions as there are people in the world.*

Yes, such a conclusion seems logical, and in a sense it is
true. We all have our personal beliefs, our peculiar ways of
looking at life. Our personal world-views always have their
unique qualities. This is what sets us apart as individuals.
But our personal idiosyncracies are usually rather superficial.
At the center of our lives we are likely to find that our fundamental attitudes and beliefs are not so different from those
of our parents, our friends, our community, and our society
as a whole. We tend to absorb the beliefs of those around
us. This very natural process or tendency is fundamental to the
growth of human societies. In the history of mankind, many
civilizations have arisen; in each we can find the existence of
a particular religion, philosophy or point of view.

TO MEET THE REAL DRAGON

Today, the world is dominated by Western civilization. Western civilization is very diverse, but at the same time, it has at its core certain characteristic viewpoints. At the heart of Western civilization, I see the existence of two very fundamental world-views. One could be charcterized as that of "traditional religion." It is based on a belief in God, spirit, and ideas in general. Philosophers usually refer to this as idealism. The second world-view might be called "anti-religion." Denying the existence of god and the importance of ideas, it bases its understanding of life on an objective study of the material world and the impersonal forces which operate in it. This is the philosophy of materialism.

These two philosophies are totally different, totally incompatible views of life. And yet they exist side by side in the heart of Western civilization. Such a situation is extremely unstable and dangerous. I believe it is the source of the confusion and chaos which characterize so much of modern life. We are torn between two utterly opposing world-views, two eternally conflicting religions. Sometimes we lean one way, sometimes another; but the choice is always painful and confusing. We long for peace but peace never comes. This is our situation, our heritage as citizens in the modern world of Western civilization.

Assuming what you say is true, what is the cause of the situation? It seems strange to me that there should be only two opposing philosophies or religions—why not five or ten?

It is a matter of history. The world, as it exists today, is the product of a very long process, a kind of evolutionary process. As I said, many civilizations have come into existence and each has been characterized by a particular religion, philosophy, or ideology. In the course of time, these civilizations have encountered one another, and through these encounters, the existence of different ways of living and thinking have become apparent. It is part of man's nature to believe that his own way of life is correct and superior. When he meets a different religion or outlook, he perceives it as something alien, something threatening to his own identity and security. At such times, a very powerful instinct comes naturally to the fore. That is the instinct to fight, to protect himself and his religion from the threat of the infidel: the believers in false gods, whether they be spiritual or material. In short, men fight for what they believe. This is a very miserable and regrettable characteristic of human beings. It would be nice if we could ignore the dark side of human nature, but the lessons of history cannot be denied. Wherever and whenever different religions and ideologies have encountered each other, the end result has been war.

In the outcomes of the great wars of history I see the working of a stern law—a law similar in many ways to the law of the survival of the fittest in nature—and, while I abhor war, I am forced to look at history objectively; I am forced to see a certain unhappy necessity in this harsh law of survival. The great wars have been turning points in the flowing river of history. In them we can clearly see the evolutionary process by which our world has been created. Through that process, two streams of thought have slowly emerged and defined themselves in opposition to each other. They have become identified with separate realms or sectors of life. Traditional religions have retained their idealistic tendencies while science and economics have turned to materialistic interpretations of existence. The idealistic and materialistic world-views which compete in the arena of Western civilization are the survivors of the historical process I have described.

Today we find ourselves caught in this highly polarized situation—a situation in which further conflict seems inevitable and, in a sense, necessary. I think the process which began so long ago will continue. There will be further competition and further clarification until, at last, human beings find the ultimate religion toward which they have been moving for so many centuries. When they have found that religion, they will be able to see and accept all philosophical viewpoints as they

are. They will be able to live in harmony with others and at
peace within themselves. They will be able to live as true
human beings at last. This is my belief.

TO MEET A TRUE MASTER

I think some of you may be meeting Buddhism for the first time. Perhaps you have read books about Zen or Buddhist philosophy. If so, you will already be familiar with some aspects of Buddhist theory. But simply to study Buddhist theory is not to meet Buddhism itself. Meeting Buddhism requires something more real than merely reading words in a book. One aspect of that "real something" is personal contact with a Buddhist teacher or master. Only through such face-to-face contact can we begin to discover what Buddhism is. So I think the first meeting with a master is very important. I remember very clearly the first time I met my Master. I'd like to tell you about it now.

I have already mentioned that I was one of those people who are naturally attracted to religion. That was, perhaps, an over-simplification. When I was young, I was very sincere and very naive. I believed quite blindly in the ideas I encountered. My parents did not believe in any particular religion, but they had a reverent attitude toward life, and I suppose they encouraged my simple-minded faith in ideas. But all that changed rather abruptly about the time I entered junior high school. The natural changes in my body at that time seemed to trigger changes in my mental outlook as well. I suddenly became skeptical of my former beliefs. It seemed that they were based on nothing more substantial than wishful thinking and a lot of mistaken notions about life. I could find no reason to do this or not to do that, and so, for a time, I lived a rather free life. I could, however, take little pleasure in my freedom. Life seemed empty and depressing. I gradually became lazier and more self-indulgent. My health began to decline.

I was rescued from my dismal state by the approach of the high school entrance examination. It was the challenge I needed to awaken my dormant energies. I applied myself to my studies, and as I did so, my life as a whole became more settled. Then I joined a track and field club and began to train for long-distance running. As a result, my health began to improve; my mind became clearer and more serene, seeming to reflect my body's renewed health and vigor. This dramatic change in my physical and mental well-being was a source of wonder to me. Was it only a coincidence? Only a matter of maturing? What, I wondered, was the relationship between the body and the mind?

This was only one of many questions which began to concern me. At that time in Japan, the rightist party predominated, and I wondered if I, as a student, should support its growing militarism. How could a person judge such matters clearly and correctly? In searching for answers to such questions, I was drawn inevitably to philosophy and religion. I read a few books about Buddhism, but they gave me the impression that Buddhism was essentially a philosophy of asceticism and self-denial. Such a pessimistic approach to life was not what I was looking for.

Then I read a book titled *A Study of the Spiritual History of Japan* by Tetsuro Watsuji. It was said to be a masterpiece which every student should read. Among the religious figures in Japanese history, I was most strongly attracted to Master Dogen, a Buddhist priest of the thirteenth century. The story of his long and ultimately successful quest for the Truth was very inspiring. I wanted to know more about this interesting man and his ideas about life. I searched for his original writings, and I found them in a book called *Shōbōgenzō*, which

means, "Essence of the Truth." At the time, I had youthful
confidence in my ability to understand whatever I wanted to
read, but to my surprise, I could understand almost nothing of
the *Shōbōgenzō*. In spite of this, I was somehow attracted to the
book. The sentences held a peculiar charm for me. I felt intuitively that they contained a thought which was fine and unusual, even though I could not grasp its meaning clearly.

About that time, I found a notice in a Buddhist magazine about
a study and practice seminar, or *sesshin*, to be held in a
temple north of Tokyo. The talks were to be given by Master
Kodo Sawaki who was a priest of the Soto sect, the school of
Japanese Buddhism which recognizes Master Dogen as its founder.
Master Sawaki was one of the better known masters in Japan at
that time. He had become famous, in part, for his style of
living and teaching which was in the ancient tradition of the
mendicant or homeless monk. He had no temple of his own, but
wandered about Japan "borrowing" temples which ordinarily
received little use. There he would stay for a while, gathering
disciples, teaching them his understanding of Buddhism, and
then move on to another temple and another group of students.
He liked to call himself "Kodo without a lodging-house." It was
this wandering life style which eventually brought Master
Sawaki to the Temple north of Tokyo, and his residence there
provided me with my first opportunity to experience a sesshin
and hear the words of a living master. I remember feeling happy
and full of anticipation as I set off for the temple with
my small bag of rice and supplies. I felt that I was embarking
on a kind of adventure: a quest for the Truth.

I was deeply impressed by Master Sawaki at that first lecture.
The subject of his talk was the *Fukan Zazengi* or *The Universal
Recommendation for Zazen*. It was Master Dogen's first major
work. In it he wrote clear and practical instructions for
zazen, the Buddhist practice of sitting in quietness, and
he also explained the essential points of Buddhist theory very
concisely. Master Sawaki talked about the opening sentences of
the work which say, "Fundamentally, the Truth exists every-

where, so how could it be dependent on practice or realization. Since the means of attaining the essence of Buddhism is abundantly present in every place, how can it be necessary to make strenuous efforts in our lives?" As Master Sawaki explained these words, I was struck by the fundamentally positive and optimistic attitude which they seemed to project. Could it be that my initial impression of Buddhism as a pessimistic religion was incorrect? As the lecture continued, I felt that Master Sawaki was communicating the essence of his more than sixty years experience. I was very moved. I felt that at last I was listening to the simple truth—that Master Kodo Sawaki was indeed a true master of Buddhism.

QUESTIONS & ANSWERS

How can we find a "true master" of Buddhism?

You must look for him.

But if we meet a Buddhist teacher, how can we know that he is a "true teacher" or a "true master"?

Generally, when we meet a teacher we will have some intuitive feeling as to whether his teachings are true or not. Having found someone whom we feel is a true teacher, the next step is to actually open ourselves to the teacher and to what he is saying. Some of those things may seem rather outrageous. The master may say that Buddha is a weed in the garden or a leaf falling from a tree. At such times we must be willing to consider the possibility: yes, perhaps Buddha is a weed or a falling leaf. Then, having considered the master's teachings with an open mind, we must test his teachings in our own lives. This is an important phase of Buddhist study. At the beginning of our Buddhist life we are usually involved in a process of trial and error. We have to find out what is true through our own efforts.

TO MEET A TRUE MASTER

Sensei, in your talk you spoke of your early introduction to Buddhism, but I am curious about your life as a whole. I read some of the details of your career on the cover of one of your books. I learned that you were a student at the University of Tokyo, that you worked for the government in the Ministry of Finance, and that you later worked for a securities firm. We generally don't associate such activities with the life of a priest. But I know that in the latter part of your life you were, in fact, ordained as a priest. So, I'm wondering what differences you found in your life after becoming a Buddhist priest. How did it change your personality and how did it affect your attitude toward other people?

Fundamentally speaking, there were no differences. My life before and after becoming a priest was the same. Before becoming a priest, I lived my real life, my Buddhist life. After becoming a priest, I continued to live my real Buddhist life. I lived my Buddhist life from day to day, from moment to moment—sometimes in my office, sometimes in my home, sometimes in a temple. In every situation there was just my Buddhist life. So we can say that becoming a priest is a kind of ceremony. It is an important ceremony, but it does not change the fundamental situation. The fundamental situation is just our Buddhist life, here and now. It does not change.

In your early life did you have the feeling of a monk?

What do you mean, "the feeling of a monk"?

Well, some people seem to have a special quality, a special attitude toward life...

Yes, I suppose I had the feeling of a monk. And I had the feeling of a layman. I had the feeling of a businessman, a father, and so on. At the same time, I had the feeling of a human being.

I'm curious about why Master Kodo Sawaki made such a strong impression on you. Why was he such a good teacher?

I think it was because his teaching was so pure. Usually, when someone does something, there is some special motive behind it, some conscious or unconscious desire to get something in re- turn for his effort. But, in Master Kodo Sawaki, I could sense no such motive. He taught simply because it was natural for him to teach. His teaching was pure and his theory was simple and clear. He urged the people who gathered around him simply to practice zazen. He said that zazen was Buddhism itself. So, although I was prone to be doubting and critical, when I heard Master Sawaki's words I could not criticize them. When I met him, I was struck by something in his manner and in his words alike. It was a kind of intuitive feeling. I felt that Master Kodo Sawaki was the embodiment of the Truth—that his teachings were the Truth itself.

Don't you feel that there was some particular quality in you which made you very receptive to Master Sawaki? You must have been a special student.

Yes, I suppose you could say that I was especially stupid.

Stupid?

Yes, stupid—stupid in a worldly sense. Clever people generally have little time for questions about the relationship between body and mind, or the nature of the Truth. But such questions were all-important to me. In some sense I was too serious, too straight or simple-minded, but I think it was that very quality which made me receptive to the Truth when I heard it. So I think the important thing is not how clever we are, but whether or not we believe in the Truth and seek it sincerely.

Why did Master Kodo Sawaki stress the importance of zazen so exclusively?

Master Sawaki had a special reverence for the practice of zazen

and he often told us how he first came to realize its importance. He was just a teenager when he decided to become a monk.
He wanted to enter the great monastery of Eihei-ji, which had
been established by Master Dogen; but to become a monk at
Eihei-ji at that time it was necessary to have the backing of
a wealthy family. Unfortunately, he had lost his parents and
was very poor, so to enter the temple he was forced to become
a servant boy for the monks. As a result, his life at the
temple was hard and uninspiring. The chief of the servants
was a stern old lady who kept her charges busy from morning
till night, cleaning and doing menial chores for the monks. Her
constant scolding echoed in his ears throughout the day, and he
found that he had no time to practice zazen, or to take part in
the other religious activities of the temple.

Then one day there was a special holiday and all the monks left
the temple to visit their families or to spend some time with
their friends. So the young servant boy found himself alone at
the temple, and he decided that it was a good opportunity for
him to practice zazen. He went to a large room and began to sit
quietly in a corner. It was dark and peaceful. After some
time the old cleaning lady came into the room singing quietly
to herself. At first she was unaware of Master Sawaki's presence, but when her eyes had adjusted to the dim light in the
room, she suddenly saw him sitting there in the corner. Falling
to her knees in astonishment, she bowed down to him again and
again. Then Master Sawaki realized that zazen had a very special power: a mystical quality which could lend authority and
grace even to a poor servant boy.

That experience was a pivotal one in Master Sawaki's life. He
resolved, then and there, to practice zazen at every opportunity. The more he practiced, the deeper his belief in the power
of zazen became. His daily practice enabled him, in time, to
comprehend the fundamental basis of Buddhist theory, and he
thus became a very excellent master. At the time he began to
teach, the true understanding of Buddhism and zazen had declined in Japan. Many priests practiced zazen only as a formal

duty, but Master Kodo Sawaki recognized the natural supremacy of zazen. He taught us the joy of practice. He reestablished zazen in Japan.

MASTER DOGEN

In the first chapter I spoke of the evolution of religions, of the competition between world views and ideologies. Such competition of ideas takes place within religions as well as between them. In this respect Buddhism is no different from other religions. Scholars and historians have traced the philosophy of Gautama Buddha as it spread from country to country and passed from generation to generation. In this process, widely varied and conflicting interpretations came into being, giving rise to the many schools and sects of Buddhism.

When Master Dogen wrote the *Fukan Zazengi* in 1228, he proclaimed the establishment of a new religion in Japan. This new religion, he declared, was Buddhism: "true Buddhism." This was a very bold statement to make. After all, Buddhism had originally appeared in Japan fully six hundred years before. There were many beautiful temples and powerful Buddhist sects in Japan when Master Dogen was born, and the sutras of ancient India were chanted daily in the monasteries of his birthplace. How then could he claim to bring a new religion to Japan? What was the source of his confidence?

This was one of many problems that bothered and intrigued me following that first sesshin with Master Kodo Sawaki. In the following years I found answers to some questions, and others arose, as I sought to understand the *Shōbōgenzō*, and the complex man who had written it so many centuries before. During those years, Master Sawaki skillfully guided and encouraged my practice and study until one day I realized that I had no more questions; the *Shōbōgenzō* had become clear, and at the same time, life itself had become very simple and direct.

When I finally understood the *Shōbōgenzō*, I could at last understand Master Dogen's claim to have brought true Buddhism to Japan. I realized that the Buddhism taught in the *Shōbōgenzō* was very different from the Buddhism taught by other priests in Japan. I understood that if Master Dogen's thought represented the true spirit and content of Gautama Buddha's teaching, then the theories of the other schools must belong to entirely different streams of thought; that they must, in fact, be different religions.

These are rather strong words, I realize, but I think it is very important to consider the problem of what "true Buddhism" is. In our lives we are bound to meet many conflicting religious and philosophical doctrines. At such times, it is very nice to be tolerant and open-minded, but on the other hand, it is also important to think critically about what they say. We must sharpen our minds. We must look closely at the theories we encounter and ask ourselves what they really mean. In this we should not be misled by labels. We should not presume that every theory and practice which claims to be Buddhism is in fact derived from the teachings of Gautama Buddha. This is very important. I am very happy that Westerners like yourselves have become interested in Buddhism. I think Buddhism has much to offer you and to Western civilization as a whole, but I fear that much of the value and the promise of Buddhism is in danger of being lost amidst a great babble of Buddhist, quasi-Buddhist and non-Buddhist voices. So now I must raise my own lonely voice and hope that it will not be lost in the din. I must do so because I believe with all my heart that Master Dogen's Buddhism is "true Buddhism," and I believe that the *Shōbōgenzō* is the best book about Buddhism in the world.

MASTER DOGEN

My aim is not to have you take sides in a great intellectual debate. My hope is only to make the philosophy of Master Dogen clear to you. Then you will be able to test the theory in your own life and come to your own conclusions regarding its truth. In the remaining chapters, I would like to introduce and explain the most important theories of Buddhism as they are taught by Master Dogen in the *Shōbōgenzō*. But if you are to understand the *Shōbōgenzō*, I think you need to know something about the life and times of the man who wrote it.

Master Dogen was born in the year A.D. 1200, a time of confusion and change in Japan. The capital had recently been moved from Kyoto, where Master Dogen was born, to Kamakura, where the government was in the hands of the military. But the royal court in Kyoto was still a center of wealth and power, and Master Dogen was born in the midst of its intrigues. His father was Michichika Kuga, a powerful minister of the court; but his mother, while also of high birth, was not Michichika's legal wife. Apparently, she had become his mistress after her first husband was exiled. So, while some aspects of Master Dogen's birth were promising, I think we can see the seeds of future misfortune in its circumstances.

When Master Dogen was only two years old, his father died quite suddenly; as a result, he became the ward of an elder brother who sent him and his mother to live in an isolated villa. There he spent the next five years, a lonely time during which he became very devoted to his mother. He is said to have been a very sensitive and intelligent child, who learned to read Chinese poetry at an early age. When Master Dogen was seven, his mother became ill and died. Her death must have made a strong and lasting impression on him. Some biographers claim that through the passing of his mother he profoundly recognized the impermanence of worldly life and the transitory nature of all things. They say that he resolved to become a monk as a result of this experience. In any case, when he was twelve years old, he ran away from his brother's house and went to Mt. Hiei, the center of Buddhist learning at the time. One year

later, over his family's objections, he became a monk at Enryaku-ji, a temple of the Tendai sect of Japanese Buddhism.

At Enryaku-ji, Master Dogen quickly immersed himself in the
study of Buddhist philosophy, but within a short time, a cru-
cial tenet of that philosophy, the doctrine of Buddha-nature,
began to trouble him. He read the words of the ancient sutra:
"Gautama Buddha said, 'All living beings without exception
have Buddha-nature; the perfect Buddha is eternal and without
change.'" If, as is said, Buddha-nature is the eternal essence
of all things, and if this essence is possessed by all people
from birth, why then, Master Dogen wondered, is it necessary
to study Buddhism at all? Why should we have to work so hard to
attain the true nature we already have?

Master Dogen took his question from one priest to another in
the monastery, but to his surprise, none of them could understand the nature of his doubt. To them, Buddha-nature was
simply an idea, so they attempted to answer his question on
theoretical grounds. But the young Master was not satisfied
with such answers. He had a very practical mind, and so he
wanted a practical answer—an answer which could resolve the
problem in terms of his own real life. Finally, in frustration,
he decided to leave the temple and seek his true master—a
master who could answer his questions without hesitation, a
master who knew the Buddha-nature itself. His search took him
eventually to Onjo-ji, where he met Master Koin. The Master
was also unable to satisfy the young man, but he suggested that
he visit a master named Eisai who had recently returned from
China.

Eisai, the founder of the Rinzai sect in Japan, was at that
time the master of Kennin-ji in Kyoto. There is some contro-
versy as to whether Master Dogen actually met Master Eisai, but
we do know that he went to Kennin-ji, and one biographer re-
lates an interesting story about the meeting between the two
Masters. He says that when Master Dogen met Eisai, he immediately put to him his question about Buddha-nature. In answer

Eisai said simply, "I know nothing of so-called Buddhas of the past, present or future; but I do know that cats and white oxen actually exist on this earth." Somehow this answer cut through Master Dogen's intellectual preoccupations and he was able to see that it is reality which is important. Whether inspired by this direct answer or by some other aspect of the new "Zen" teachings of Eisai, Master Dogen decided to stay at Kennin-ji to continue his training. Unfortunately, Master Eisai died shortly after Master Dogen took up residence at the temple, so he became the student of Master Myozen, Eisai's successor.

Master Myozen was an excellent teacher who sought after the Truth very diligently. Master Dogen was impressed by that sincere will to attain the Truth, and he worked hard to follow his Master's example. At Kennin-ji, the traditional Tendai doctrines were taught alongside the new Zen teachings introduced by Eisai, but it was the latter, with their emphasis on the direct apprehension of reality, which had the most appeal for Master Dogen. After almost nine years of strenuous study and practice, Master Dogen became convinced that if he were ever to penetrate to the core of Zen, he would have to journey to its source in China. Master Myozen was also taken by the idea, so in 1223, the two monks made the hazardous voyage to China together.

At first, Master Dogen found China a disappointment. He visited many temples but found that their masters were more concerned with wealth and position than with practice. He had almost decided to give up his search when he met an old man who told him of Master Tendō Nyojō, a famous priest who had recently become the master of Tendo-zan Keitoku-ji. The old man's eagerness to have him meet Tendō Nyojō convinced Master Dogen to visit the temple. At their first encounter, Master Dogen felt intuitively that Master Nyojō was the "True Master" he had been searching for so long. Master Nyojō, in turn, felt that the young Japanese monk standing before him was just the man he had been waiting for to carry on his teachings.

TO MEET THE REAL DRAGON

So Master Dogen became the disciple of Master Nyojō, and within a rather short time, his doubts were cleared away. He understood the real basis of Buddhist theory and realized the Truth with his whole body and mind. Four years after coming to China, Master Dogen received the formal transmission of the Buddhist teachings from Master Nyojō, and so took his place in the direct line of masters which stretches back to Gautama Buddha himself. He was twenty-seven years old.

Having attained his goal in China, Master Dogen decided to go back to Japan to transmit the true teachings of Gautama Buddha to his native land. He first returned to Kennin-ji, and it was there that he wrote the *Fukan Zazengi*, his first important work on the practice of zazen. He found, however, that the spirit of discipline and sencerity at the temple had declined greatly during his stay in China. So, after a few years, he moved to a small temple outside Kyoto and began to give lectures to a group of monks and laymen. Among those students was one named Ejo. To Ejo, Master Dogen entrusted the task of recording his lectures. These recorded lectures were the starting point of the *Shōbōgenzō*: Master Dogen's great effort to preserve his understanding of Buddhism for future generations.

When we read the *Shōbōgenzō* today, we are usually struck by its great breadth and complexity. It delves deeply into the most profound problems of life and considers those problems from many seemingly contradictory standpoints. Its depth and complicated structure tend, at first, to obscure the fact that, at its core, Master Dogen's thought is very simple and practical. He teaches us that the ultimate meaning of Buddhism is to be found not in theory, but in the practice of zazen. For him, Buddhism and zazen are fundamentally one and the same thing: to practice zazen is Buddhism itself. Buddhism is to practice zazen.

This radical reduction of Buddhist theory to its simplest and most essential basis was very attractive to many people. They came to his lectures in ever increasing numbers. As his fame spread, the established sects became jealous of his influence and began to interfere with his work. Finally Master Dogen decided to move once more, this time to a remote district north of Kyoto. There he established a temple he called Eihei-ji, or the Temple of Eternal Peace. It is now the main temple of the Soto sect in Japan.

In 1252, after teaching many disciples, Master Dogen became ill and returned to Kyoto where he died in 1253.

QUESTIONS & ANSWERS

I am interested in the problem of Buddha-nature. I'm not sure I understand the story of Master Dogen's question about Buddha-nature. What is Buddha-nature, anyway?

From the standpoint of ultimate Truth, we can say that Buddha-nature is simply nature as it is, the universe as it is, ourselves as we are. But in the story of young Master Dogen we must realize that, to him, Buddha-nature was something other than this world, here and now. Being young and intelligent, it was quite natural for him to form an intellectual concept of Buddha-nature: to imagine the existence of something of an immaterial nature, something which could be neither seen nor felt, yet which was possessed by all beings without exception. It seems likely that he thought of Buddha-nature as a kind of spiritual essence. His idea was perhaps similar in many ways to the Christian concept of souls. Having formed this intellectual concept of Buddha-nature, Master Dogen was then faced with the practical meaning of Buddha-nature in his life. The scriptures urged him to seek the Buddha-nature, to find it, to realize it. But if Buddha-nature really resides in all beings, how could it be necessary to seek it? There was something contradictory or illogical in this idea, and this contradiction was, I think, the crux of Master Dogen's problem.

The other priests at the temple also had only a theoretical

concept of Buddha-nature, so they couldn't answer his question. But when he met Master Eisai, he found a master whose understanding of Buddhism was based on reality itself. Eisai answered the question with a statement about his own life, his own experience. He had no special knowledge of Buddhas or Buddha-nature, but what he saw in this world, he really saw: cats and white oxen—they actually existed. In his life Buddhism was not some kind of idealistic theory. It was life itself. He was a simple man in this world: a Buddha.

And so, as the story goes, Master Dogen was very inspired, and he studied Buddhism for many years in Japan and China until he finally attained enlightenment, or realized the Truth—or something—I'm not sure what. I have also read many other stories about great Buddhist masters who practiced very hard and lived alone in caves, or sat facing a wall for nine years. It is really interesting. They are beautiful stories, and I enjoy reading them, but unfortunately, I can't really relate their experience to my own life. I can't imagine doing the same thing myself. I'm too weak.

I think there are two problems here. The first is the nature of the stories themselves. The fact is that such stories are just stories—not real life. Stories always tend to become more interesting and attractive when they are told again and again. So we read such stories and we feel very inspired—uplifted. We want to believe in something fantastic or extraordinary so we tend to be too gullible. We should be more critical, I think. We should remember that stories are stories.

When we look at the stories more objectively, we begin to see that the stories are about real people after all, ordinary people like ourselves. But even from this standpoint, we must admit that people have made very strenuous efforts and endured extreme hardships in their practice. This brings us to the second problem. Why have people made such extreme efforts? I think the reason is that they were looking for something which is not in this world. They wanted something which is not in this universe. They searched and practiced ever more diligently until, at last, they realized that they need not look for anything. This was, for them, the experience of the so-called satori: the experience of life as it is.

The sudden awakening to the fact that we need not search for anything is a very profound experience for many people. They have made fantastic efforts, and at last they have seen something of the Truth. Unfortunately, such people are likely to see the strenuous quality of their efforts as the cause of their awakening. They may then become even more zealous. They want to tell the world of their experience. Quite naturally, they urge us to follow the same path. They tell us that we must be willing to break our bones and crush the marrows if we are finally to reach the great enlightenment. They encourage us to seek the very dream which obscured their vision for so long. It is ironic, and it is an irony with a tragic consequence, for the majority of people do not have the single-minded will to follow such a path. They are at first attracted by fantastic stories. Then they try to emulate their heroes, but they are soon confronted by their own weakness: "My master sat facing the wall for nine years, but I can't sit for nine minutes. My karma must be too strong. I must be a hopeless case." Thus they become discouraged as quickly as they were inspired. They are defeated before they begin, and they lose the will to attain the Truth. It is a tragedy.

So when we read stories of priests and masters of ancient times, we need not be awed, nor need we hesitate to begin our own practice. They had their lives and we have ours. They were not so strong and we are not so weak. The point is that we must work with our own situation.

It's easy to understand, intellectually, that we need not search for anything, but somehow that's not enough, is it? We really have to work extraordinarily hard to realize the Truth, don't we?

It's an interesting question. The fundamental task in Buddhism is to regain our original composure, our original state. It is to enter a balanced state of body and mind. Master Dogen often said that to crush our bones and marrows may be difficult, but it is more difficult to regulate the state of our mind. So the question is, what is the best way to regulate our mind? Dramatic and severe practices are interesting, but I think they have little effect in the long run. Master Dogen taught us that the best way to regulate our mind is to practice zazen every day. If we practice zazen every day, we can enter the state of Buddha, and the state will never leave us. To continue to practice every day is difficult, but it is never impossible. So to attain the Truth is not so easy and it is not so difficult. It is only as difficult as continuing the practice of zazen every day.

But I have real problems in my life. I still don't understand how I can find the strength to solve them, much less to regulate my mind. I really do feel weak.

To feel weak is natural. When we first begin to practice, we feel weak because we are weak. But the practice itself begins to give us strength and vitality. It has a kind of snowballing effect—not in a dramatic way, but very gradually and steadily, we become stronger. Then one day we find that what seemed impossible before, we are now doing very naturally every day.

Of course we all have our particular problems in life, and we must do whatever is necessary to overcome them. But I think we need not regard our problems as "the enemy." In fact, we should realize that it is our problems in life which give us the motivation or will to seek the Truth in the first place. Recently, one of my students told me about some of the painful experiences of his childhood. I told him that his pain had awakened him and made him want to find the Truth. He told me later that my simple answer had touched him and given him a new outlook, not only on his past, but also on his problems in the present. I think this is very important. If we can change the way we perceive our problems, the problems themselves will change. They will cease to be problems. They will become our inspiration.

Our problems may give us the inspiration to look for the Truth, but it seems to me that very few people actually find it. In the case of Master Dogen, what gave him the will to follow through—to actually do it?

According to Buddhist theory, the Truth exists in each of us— not only within us, but in every place and in every situation. So the most important thing is to awaken the desire to find this fundamental Truth. In Master Dogen we can see that this will to find or attain the Truth was very strong. There are perhaps many reasons for this, but I think the major ones are revealed in his biography.

To begin with, he was very intelligent and sensitive, so he was quick to perceive the true qualities of his world. That world was especially confused. The royal court in Kyoto had all the trappings of power and influence, but in fact had no real power at all. It was essentially a sham, and I think Master Dogen sensed this and was repelled by it. The early death of his mother was a shock, but I feel that the more important effect of her absence was that it filled him with longing: a longing for something most of us find in the touch of our mother's skin, but which, in Master Dogen, became a longing for the Truth. So this feeling of longing, coupled with his feelings of disgust for the social world around him, led him to the temples and monasteries near his home. There he practiced zazen, and it was the power of zazen itself which eventually carried him to the realization of the Truth.

A WORLD DIVIDED

What is Buddhism? That is our problem. What is the Truth? That is also our problem. What is reality or the real world? What is a Buddha or a Buddhist master? What is the meaning of zazen, Buddhist theory, the realization of the Truth? The questions are beginning to pile up, aren't they? You've heard suggestions of this, hints of that, but so far, everything must seem rather vague. Perhaps you are beginning to feel a bit restless. Just what is Buddhism, anyway?

Well, it is very difficult, if not impossible, to explain what Buddhism is in just a few words. I could offer a definition of Buddhism, but I'm afraid my definition would only raise more questions in your mind. You could read my words, but you would not really be sure what I was saying. So at this point, we have a problem. It is a problem of words and meanings, a problem of communication. I think that the first step in studying any religion, theory, or philosophy is to establish an intellectual basis or foundation, a common ground for communication. Establishing such a basis may seem a difficult task, but I think it can be accomplished, for as a Buddhist, I believe that we are all living in the same world—that, on a fundamental level, we all share the same experience of life and the same ways of seeing and understanding the world in which are living. In other words, I feel that the common ground for communication

already exists—that the only problem is to bring the situation, as it is, into sharper focus. To do so, we should look
clearly into the simplest, most fundamental aspects of our
lives. If we can gain some insights into the ways we see and
understand ourselves and the world, then I think we will have
the intellectual tools we need to understand what Buddhism is.

So, shall we study ourselves? Shall we investigate our world?
It sounds like a good idea, but how can we actually do it? How
can we begin?

We might begin by asking ourselves what we are doing right now,
and what we do every day. For most of us, waking up in the
morning is the starting point of our day-to-day life. We are
often jolted from our dreams by the alarm clock. We shut it off
automatically, then lie quietly collecting ourselves. We begin
to think...

"What's that noise? Is it raining? Oh no, it is raining! I
wonder where I left my umbrella. Oh, I hate rainy days. What
time is it? Ten past eight. Getting late. Must get up."

We stretch, wiggle our toes. The bed is nice and cozy.

"Oh, do I have to get up? Maybe just five minutes more sleep
will make the day go better. Let's see, what was I going to do
today anyway..."

Our minds are moving quickly now—jumping from thought to
thought, worry to worry. We may spend the next ten minutes like
this—talking with ourselves, encouraging ourselves to get up,
until finally, at some moment, we actually do it—we get up. We
stumble to the bathroom. We wash our faces. While we are brush-
ing our teeth, we consider the problem of breakfast.

"What shall I have today? Yesterday it was eggs, how about pancakes today? Yes, I definitely deserve pancakes on a day like
this."

A WORLD DIVIDED

And so it goes. How much time has passed since the alarm clock rang? Twenty minutes? One hour? What were we doing all that time? What did we actually do? We opened our eyes. We got out of bed. We brushed our teeth. Not very much really. It seems that most of the time we were thinking—just thinking. In fact, most of us spend most of the time doing just that—just thinking. We think of the future, remember the past, worry about this and that. Our minds are constantly active, constantly flitting from thought to thought, like butterflies in a field of flowers.

At other times, our thoughts take on another quality. They build on each other, becoming ever more involved and complex. We formulate grand theories and create interesting stories involving those we love and hate. We often catch ourselves awakening from sweet reveries, wish-fulfilling daydreams, or dramatic melodramas. It seems that our minds can create complete worlds: worlds of fantasy and illusion—worlds in which we can finally tell the boss what we really think of him. In the realm of thought, we can realize our fondest dreams. But of course, dreams are only dreams...

Most of us realize the illusory nature of our daydreams, but we rarely question the nature of thought itself. We are so accustomed to thinking that it never occurs to us to question what we are doing. Thinking is such an important facet of our day-to-day lives that living and thinking seem almost synonomous. We lose sight of the difference between the real world and thinking about the world. In fact, our world, our reality, becomes the world of thinking itself. We live in the world of thinking.

Few of us, however, are completely lost in thought. We generally find confirmation for our visions of reality through contact with the external world. We feel the warmth of our beds, the tingle of a cold shower. We inhale the fragrance of freshly brewed coffee; enjoy the taste of bacon and eggs. These are pleasant things, reliable things. We need not doubt their existence. The world we can touch and feel is a secure world, a more substantial world than the world of thinking.

For many people, this realm of the senses is reality itself. They scorn idle thinking and dreaming and seek the security of possessions and the pleasures of sensory experience. This, then, is the world of things and sensation. It is the world of feeling. The world of feeling is the other side of the world of thinking.

Can you recognize the existence of these two worlds, the worlds of thinking and feeling? I think that on a very simple and intuitive level, we are all aware of this division in our lives. It seems very natural to divide that which we think from that which we feel. Thinking belongs to the realm of the mind, while feeling is bound to the body and the material world. Mind and body, as we usually conceive of them, are separate and distinct entities with very different functions and characteristics. Mind is something vague and intangible. Lacking the definite qualities of matter, it is sometimes thought of as a kind of ethereal substance or energy, something akin to spirit. Mind is thus rather mysterious and mystical, perhaps eternal. Body, on the other hand, is substantial—material. It is subject to the strict laws of nature. It grows, whithers, and dies. The body is mortal. It is basically animal in nature.

With slight variations, people at the heart of Western civilization, as well as those who later came under its influence, have accepted and held fast to this fundamental conception of the division between mind and body for many, many centuries. From the time of the ancient Greeks, and perhaps even before, philosophers have worried over the problem of body and mind. It is interesting to note, however, that the questions have generally been concerned with the exact relationship between body and mind. Such questions presuppose the validity of the division itself. They assume that there is indeed a real difference between body and mind.

A WORLD DIVIDED

It seems likely that cultures isolated from the stream of Western civilization had quite different views of reality. We might say that they failed to see the difference between body and mind. That sounds strange, doesn't it? How could they miss such a fundamental distinction? The body is here, right here. It is made of flesh and blood and bones. On the other hand, something is happening which is obviously not flesh and bones. We are thinking. We have these marvelous images, these very intricate thoughts going on all the time. Maybe we don't understand it exactly, but at least we can be sure that the mind exists. It does exist, doesn't it? We are sure, aren't we?

Well, I'm not so sure. I think I mentioned earlier that I became interested in the relationship between body and mind when I was quite young, so when I began to study the *Shōbōgenzō*, I was particularly interested in discovering Master Dogen's attitude toward the problem. I found that his point of view was quite different from anything I had read before. I couldn't understand his thought clearly at first, but at some point I realized that he often spoke of the mental and the physical as if they were one thing. He seemed to be saying that the mind and the body were not two things having a special, intricate relationship, but two faces of one indivisible reality; that when we look at life from one side, we perceive the body; and when we change our perspective, we become aware of thought: we discover the mind.

I later realized that this was not a theory peculiar to Master Dogen, but one of the axioms of Buddhist philosophy. From the time of Gautama Buddha himself, Buddhist masters have insisted that the mind and the body are one. From the Buddhist standpoint, our usual interpretation of body and mind is only that: an interpretation, an assumption we make about reality. Such assumptions are hard to shake. They are a matter of common sense. Common sense tells us that the body and the mind really do exist. To think in terms of body and mind is natural and necessary. It is only common sense.

TO MEET THE REAL DRAGON

The common-sense division of body and mind is only one of many such assumptions we tend to make about our world. Generally, when we think about the world, we divide it into two parts: on one side is nature, and on the other side is man and his civilization.

We usually think of nature as the primordial world, the basic stuff of the universe. It is the combined form of matter and energy, or the accumulated result of the interaction of matter and energy. Thus, we generally feel that nature is apart from man. It has no meaning, no intelligence, no quality of spirit. It is basically inhuman. It is just there. It is there to be used, exploited, consumed. Nature has great power, so it must be respected. We must try to control it, to make it safe for us, to make it safe for mankind. We can observe that we have succeeded to a large extent. We have created the unnatural world of man in the midst of nature. We have created our civilization. Civilization is the product of our intelligence, the result of our thinking.

Usually we are very proud of our creation. Our art, literature, and science are very impressive. Man has many talents. He has created a fantastic world. Yet, we dare not look at that world too closely. If we do, we are likely to find ugliness, hatred, and war. Something is wrong with man's creation. If we consider this aspect of civilization and compare it to the natural world, we might be forced to alter our original view of nature. We might see that nature has a quality of harmony and rightness which seems to be lacking in the unnatural world of man.

When we take a walk in the woods, we often sense that harmony. The peace and quiet of nature seem to communicate something to us. Isn't that interesting? Isn't is interesting that nature— that accumulation of meaningless matter and energy—should have such an effect on us? Could it be that the division between man and nature is an artificial one, a convenient intellectual model which somehow became accepted as fact? Could it be that our common-sense view is again only an interpretation?

A WORLD DIVIDED

Our common-sense views of reality often seem to create problems for us. We see things as separate, and then the relationship between them becomes problematic. Our bodies demand food and other forms of sensory gratification. We also have certain aims, certain intellectual or religious beliefs. The two often seem to conflict. Many religions appear to regard the body as something defiled—an impure vessel for the mind or the spirit. They urge us to exalt the spirit, to give it wings so that it can soar above this trivial world. We must cut our attachment to the body, the body which is bound to the earth, nature, and the material world.

Such viewpoints are hard for many people to accept. They enjoy eating, drinking, making love. They revel in the world of the senses. To deny that world is simply to deny reality itself. So the stage seems set for conflict: conflict between people and conflict within people. The conflicts appear to arise, in part, from our view of a world divided. In fact our usual understanding of the world is rooted in duality. There is mind and body, thinking and feeling, spirit and matter, heaven and earth—the list goes on and on. When we see the pervasiveness of this interpretation, we might ask why. Why do we see the world in this way?

I think the answer is quite simple. We see things the way we do because of the nature of thinking itself. Generally speaking, we cannot think about one thing, nor can we perceive one thing in isolation. There must always be two. "This" must always be seen or considered in relation to "that." If "that" does not exist, then "this" cannot exist either. So the activity of intellect at its most basic level is to *find* differences. The mind divides, cleaves, breaks down, and rearranges. We seek to understand things by seeing them in contrast to other things. We separate the world into parts and oppose one part to another in our minds.

This is a very powerful technique. Through the centuries, man—especially Western man—has been refining this technique ever more thoroughly and exactly. To a large extent our progress in philosophy, science, and technology has come as a result of the the development of the thinking faculty in Western civiliza- tion. Most of the world is now a part of that civilization: a civilization based on the assumption of duality.

The divisions in our world view are so firmly rooted in our consciousness that they seem natural, basic, and obvious. We believe there is mind. We believe there is body. We believe they are different things. To question these beliefs seems to fly in the face of all reason and common sense.

Common sense, as I have used it here, is something more than down-to-earth thinking or practical judgement. It is the view of reality which arises from the exercise of such judgement. This common-sense view of life is not absolute, but a product of history and habit. It is the habitual view, the common view. That which is only common sense today may have been unheard of only a hundred years ago. Buddhism challenges the common-sense view of reality, or perhaps I should say, Buddhism challenges our belief in the common-sense view. Buddhism claims that the common-sense view is just that: a viewpoint, a way of thinking or understanding. It may be very useful and efficient, but it is not reality itself. Body and mind are not two sub- stances, but one. Man and nature are but two sides of the same thing. That one thing is reality. That one thing is the real situation in our lives.

QUESTIONS & ANSWERS

You seem to suggest that our dualistic understanding of reality comes out of our perception of the opposing worlds of thinking and feeling. From the Buddhist point of view, do these worlds actually exist?

No, to speak of the worlds of thinking and feeling is only to give names to very simple and ordinary ways of understanding reality. Different people have different ways of seeing the world and interpreting what they see. Some perceive thinking and ideas as real. Others believe only in the evidence of their senses. Such beliefs and interpretations are, from the Buddhist point of view, a kind of delusion. From the Buddhist stand-point, there is only one world, only one reality; but at the same time, we must recognize the existence of our one-sided or delusive interpretations of that reality. We must study the ways we actually see and interpret the real world. Such inter-pretations are very important and very powerful. They are the basis of our common-sense views of life.

Must we reject common sense?

No, I don't think so. Sometimes common sense is accurate and true. Sometimes it is distorted and false. Common-sense views of reality are products of our history and traditions, both the history of our society and our personal history. Our under-standing of the world has its cultural basis, and it is also influenced by our experiences in the world. We begin to learn the prevailing view of reality as soon as we are born. As we grow older, this prevailing view becomes more and more famil-iar; our thoughts and perceptions settle into the comfortable grooves of established patterns; our responses to the world become rigid and predictable. We begin to see things in habit-ual patterns rather than directly and simply, as they are. So we must recognize that our common-sense views are limited and sometimes distorted interpretations of reality. We need not reject them; but at the same time, we should realize that, at times, they may not be very reliable.

Dualistic concepts like body and mind may be a kind of delu-sion, but it is difficult to see how we can talk about our experience without resorting to such concepts.

Yes, it is true that we need our dualistic concepts in order to talk about our experience from certain points of view, but we should remember that there are other ways of interpreting the same experience.

For example...

Well, let's see...are you hungry now?

No, I just had lunch.

So, you feel full and content now, don't you?

Yes, I do.

Good! Then I think that if we were to analyze your situation according to our usual understanding of body and mind, we would say something like this: Before lunch your stomach was empty. The empty stomach caused certain physical feelings which eventually became conscious. You were then hungry. Hunger, thus understood, is a complex mental event caused by an empty stomach. After you ate lunch, your stomach produced feelings which you interpreted mentally as fullness, contentment, or satisfaction.

From the Buddhist point of view, this interpretation is too complex, too causal. For a Buddhist, the relationship between an empty stomach and hunger is more direct. An empty stomach is hunger itself. A full stomach is contentment itself. The situation, at the moment of the present, is a simple fact, a unitary fact. It is not a question of a physical cause producing a mental effect. Your stomach is full and you feel content. Fundamentally there is only one situation. Only our perspective changes—only our point of view.

But if we had'nt eaten we would still feel hungry, wouldn't we? You aren't denying the cause and effect relationship between eating and satisfying hunger, are you?

No, of course not. When we consider a chain of events in time, we must acknowledge cause and effect. But to consider cause and effect is a kind of intellectual exercise, not a matter of our moment-by-moment experience in the real world. I was speaking of a momentary situation. Right now your stomach is full. Right now you feel content. That is the situation. There is only one situation, not two. But here we are getting ahead of ourselves. We will return to the problem of cause and effect a little further on in our discussions...OK?

Could you say something more about the Buddhist attitude toward nature?

In the *Shōbōgenzō* there are several chapters in which Master Dogen discusses the Buddhist view of nature. One of them is titled "Sansui-gyo" or "Nature as Buddhist Scripture." In it we read the words: "Nature, here and now, is speaking the words of Ancient Buddhas." In another chapter we find similar words: "The sounds of valley streams are the voice of Gautama Buddha—the figures of mountains are his perfect body." I think these words express very clearly the Buddhist attitude toward nature. Buddhism regards nature as meaning-full. It is not only matter and energy. It has a certain quality which speaks to us directly—something which speaks to us of what we are, what reality is. Thus, nature teaches us the Truth. It contains the teachings of Gautama Buddha.

How can we find the teachings of Buddha in nature?

It's very simple really. When you are looking at a flower, don't you see its beauty? When you are enjoying a walk in the country, don't you feel the beauty of nature all around you?

Yes, of course—but there is nothing special about that, is there? Nature is beautiful.

Yes, nature is beautiful—and that beauty itself is the teaching of Gautama Buddha. He taught us how wonderful it is to live in this real world. The beauty of nature always reminds us of that fact; it is always sending us messages from Gautama Buddha. But, as you say, it is nothing special. The messages are not in some secret code. The beauty of nature is right here in front of our eyes. We don't have to think about it. We need not ask why nature is beautiful. We need only see it—feel it— experience it fully. When we do, we can find Buddha's teachings everywhere in the world...at every moment.

I can't see why a feeling for the beauty of nature is necessarily opposed to the common-sense view of nature as the material world. Couldn't the external world be beautiful because it is different from the world of mind or spirit?

That's an interesting notion, but based on my own experience I can't believe it is true. I think we find nature beautiful because we share something with nature or have something in common with nature. When we are in nature, we have an intuitive sense of the harmony between ourselves and the natural world. I think the fact that we can find beauty in the natural world shows that we human beings and nature are part of one broad, ineffable totality. In Buddhism we call that totality *Dharma*.

Then is it possible to realize the Buddhist Truth in nature?

Yes, there are many stories in the Buddhist scriptures about masters who attained the Truth in nature. In the chapter of the *Shōbōgenzō* which I mentioned earlier, Master Dogen comments on several of those stories. One of them is about a monk named Kyogen Chikan who studied Buddhism in the order of Master Isan Reiyu in China.

One day the Master said to the monk, "You have a very nice understanding of Buddhist theory, but please explain the Buddhist Truth to me without using words from the books you have read."

The monk could say nothing. He suddenly realized that although he had read many books about Buddhism, he had actually understood nothing. He felt very ashamed. He burnt his books and became a server of meals at the temple. After living this simple life for some time, he said to his master, "My body and mind are stupid; I cannot say anything which explains the Buddhist Truth. Please Master, give me some words to explain Buddhism."

But Master Isan Reiyu refused, saying, "It would not be difficult for me to give you some words, but if I did so, you would regret it in the future."

So the monk, Chikan, went to a place in the mountains and built a little cottage where he lived alone. His only companions were the bamboo he planted near his house. One day, as he was sweeping the path, a pebble struck the trunk of a bamboo. At the moment of hearing the sound, he attained the Truth.

Prostrating himself in the direction of his Master's temple he said, "Great Master Isan Reiyu, if you had given me words to explain Buddhism, I could never have attained the Truth. The striking of a stone on bamboo has broken my consciousness. Now I am living in the real world. I need not worry that my actions are right or wrong, and I can never fall into the state of darkened mind again."

Here is another story.

Master Rei-un Shigon studied Buddhism for thirty years. One day he took a walk in the mountains. It was spring and the peach trees were in bloom. After walking for some time, he stopped to rest at the foot of a mountain. He looked below and saw a great field of peach blossoms spreading away from him in all directions. Suddenly he realized that the world, at that very moment, was splendid and beautiful. He recognized that, moment-by-moment, he was living in the real world. He knew that, from that time on, he need not pursue the Truth; it was always with him.

After this experience, he said, "I sought the Truth for thirty

years. Many times the leaves fell from the trees and many times
they sprang out from the branches again, but when I saw the
field of beautiful peach blossoms I came into the Now. And all
my doubts vanished."

Such stories tell us that the Truth is always present in nature
and we can awaken to it at any moment. It is always there. It
is always here.

*Is the realization of the Truth always so dramatic and clear?
Is it possible to have a cloudy glimpse of the Truth?*

In actual fact, the experiences of these masters were probably
not so sharp and clear, but storytellers are prone to dramatize
events for the sake of the story. So, to answer your question,
yes, of course our experience of the Truth may not be so clear
and dramatic. Everyone has some experience of reality. As we
practice and study, our vision may clear very slowly and subtly. Then one day we may find that we have been in the midst of
reality all the time; our doubts have vanished like mist in the
morning sun.

*Your talk today makes it clear that Buddhism regards man as a
part of nature. Are we to understand, then, that Buddhism is,
at the most fundamental level, a kind of naturalism or worship
of nature?*

No, I don't think so. Buddhism recognizes our intimate connection with the natural world, and so we revere it as one beautiful face of reality; but at the same time, Buddhism recognizes
that reality has other faces. Man has his intellect. He can
think. He can act with the intention of changing his world. He
can create an unnatural world. That unnatural world is also one
face of reality. So as Buddhists, we revere nature and society
as two faces of one reality. Within that one reality, we find
our usual life. Our usual life combines nature and man's created world. It combines the material and mental aspects of
life. In Buddhism we revere our life itself.

A WORLD DIVIDED

A priest asked his master, "What is Buddhism?" The master replied, "To wear clothes and to eat meals." Another master said, "Buddhism is carrying water for your cooking. It is gathering firewood to build a cooking fire." These words have no hidden meaning. They express the fundamental attitude of Buddhism directly. True Buddhism is nothing other than our usual life.

SCIENCE AND BUDDHISM

In the last chapter we talked about our characteristic ways of
looking at the world, about our habitual or common-sense views
of reality. We discussed our tendency to divide or split
reality into parts. In contrast to that tendency, I emphasized
the Buddhist insistence on the oneness of the real world. In
the process, I may have given you the impression that Buddhism
is anti-intellectual: that Buddhism has little regard for that
faculty in human beings which divides and analyzes. If so, I
must apologize. Buddhism esteems the intellect. The ability to
think, to reason, to create and compare theoretical systems is
one of the most outstanding characteristics of human beings. We
are thinking beings. That is our nature. To deny this fact
would be foolish indeed. So Buddhism honors the intellect and
the products of that intellect: the theories of science and the
other branches of human learning. At the same time, Buddhism
insists that the theories be recognized for what they are; that
is, as tools for understanding the world. Reality itself is not
theory. Theories can never be reality.

I think this attitude is of tremendous importance in the modern
world. I feel that the Buddhist view of reality can bring a
sense of balance or perspective to our philosophical and scientific investigations. At the same time, I think that those
investigations can be of great value in clarifying the meaning

of Buddhist theory. Unfortunately, the world as a whole has yet to reap the benefits of such an exchange of views, but my personal experience convinces me that the potential for a mutually beneficial dialogue does definitely exist. So now, as an illustration of this potential, I would like to tell you a story from my own life. Through this example I hope that you will gain some appreciation of how Buddhism and science may meet, exchange views, and in the process, shed new light on the confusing contours of reality. As the starting point for this discussion, I would like to return to the problem of body and mind.

In Western science, the study of the body has traditionally been separate from the study of the mind. Physiology is the study of the physical body; psychology is the study of the mind. Of course the two fields overlap, and nowadays many doctors and psychologists are clearly aware of the interlocking nature of their specialities. Nevertheless, researchers in physiology and psychology have traditionally felt the objects of their study to be distinctly different.

I am not a physiologist or a psychologist, but my early interest in the relationship between body and mind led me to read many books on those subjects. In the process I discovered many facts and theories which helped me understand the Buddhist conception of reality. For example, ancient Buddhist scriptures contain an elaborate theory about the structure and functioning of the mind. This theory distinguishes between eight kinds of consciousness. The first five refer to the perceptions of the five senses, the sixth and seventh to those centers of the mind which organize sensory and intellectual activity, and the eighth to some rather vague "storehouse" of consciousness from which the "seeds" of our conscious thoughts and mental images were said to arise. This eighth kind of consciousness was called the *ālaya-vijñāna* in Sanskrit. In my early readings of the Buddhist scriptures and commentaries, I could find no really satisfactory explanation of what the *ālaya-vijñāna* was, or how it actually functioned. Many scholars advanced their own interpretations, but, perhaps because the *ālaya-vijñāna* was something beyond the realm of ordinary experience, these interpretations were always very abstract and sometimes quite fanciful.

Then I began to read about Dr. Sigmund Freud's investigations into what he called the unconscious. His theory was somewhat difficult to grasp, but it was at least supported by some concrete evidence, some direct observations of the ways people think and act. As I read about those observations, I gradually began to understand the basis of Freud's theory, and, through that understanding, the theory of the *ālaya-vijñāna* began to take on new meaning for me. It occurred to me that the same mental phenomena, which Freud discovered and explained by way of the unconscious mind, might have been well-known to the Buddhist masters who created the concept of *ālaya-vijñāna* to explain their observations of the mental process.

Having made this connection between Freudian psychology and Buddhist theory, I continued to look for other theories which might help to clarify my understanding. But, while the theory of the unconscious had been very helpful to me, many of Freud's ideas were difficult for me to comprehend. I couldn't understand, for example, his insistence on the preeminent importance of the sexual drive, the libido.

Then I found a series of books by a Freudian psychologist named Karl Menninger. Dr. Menninger wrote in clear and simple language and illustrated his ideas with many case histories. He explained that, at first, Freud had attempted to explain human behavior by way of a theory of instinct, which he called the libido. This basic instinct was present in the motivation of all human behavior. It took many forms, but was basically sexual in nature. According to Dr. Menninger, Freud later came to see that the libido theory was insufficient to explain many of the destructive and aggressive aspects of life. He therefore supplemented the libido theory with a thantos theory. Thus, Freud's mature theory of human motivation contained the idea that the unconscious human mind is directed by an interaction of two opposing instincts, one toward life and the other toward death.

In expressing his own understanding, Dr. Menninger preferred to characterize the two forces in human life as love and hate. He described hate as the aggressive instinct: the active, volitional and intellectual side of our nature. Love, on the other hand, was passive and sensual. It was the protective and perceptive instinct in human beings. According to Dr. Menninger, the task of our life was to find a balance between these two forces. He suggested that most of the problems of mankind could be traced to imbalances in the constructive and destructive energies of individuals and societies.

This simple idea struck me very forcefully. I felt that the theory expressed a very fundamental truth. As I thought about the idea of two conflicting instincts in our lives, and the need for harmonizing the two, many previously unrelated ideas began to come together in my mind. I thought of the Buddhist concept of *Jo*, which means the state of balanced body. Master Dogen often said that the state of balanced body was the standard state of human beings; that entering such a state was the aim of Buddhist life itself. Could the harmonizing of the forces of love and hate in the unconscious, which Dr. Menninger described as the task of our life, be the same as the aim of Buddhist life, the attainment of balanced body: the state of *Jo*?

It was an intriguing idea. I felt very inspired. At the same time, I recognized that some difficulties remained in reconciling the two theories. Dr. Menninger was a psychologist, and as such it was natural for him to think in terms of mental factors, mental instincts and forces. The theory he explained was thus a theory of mind. But in Buddhism we do not isolate the mind. In Buddhism we must always remember the combined nature of body and mind. I felt, therefore, that if we discovered a pair of opposing forces in looking at one side of life, then we should find the same phenomena when we studied the other side. In other words, I felt that the psychological manifestations of love and hate must have a physical correlary; that somewhere in the body, a physical system mirroring the psychological interaction of love and hate must exist.

In searching for that physical system, my attention was drawn again and again to the autonomic nervous system. The autonomic nervous system, as you probably know, is the division of the nervous system which regulates the internal organs and systems of the body. It works to maintain a state of equilibrium, or balance, in the functioning of those systems; this balance is achieved through the action of two separate nerve systems: the sympathetic and parasympathetic nervous systems.

As I read about the action of these two systems, I was struck by the fact that their effects on the internal organs were usually contradictory in nature. The sympathetic nervous system generally caused excitation or tension, while the parasympathetic system usually had the opposite effect. Thus, depending on the relative strength of the two systems, differing bodily states were produced, and these states were often accompanied by certain subjective or emotional feelings. At some point, then, it occurred to me that the bodily states which arise naturally through the interaction of the two sides of the autonomic nervous system might be the physical correlary of the psychological states which Freud and Menninger ascribed to the interaction of love and hate. Perhaps the functioning of the autonomic nervous system, which is ordinarily beyond our conscious control, was none other than the functioning of the unconscious itself: the *ālaya-vijñāna*.

Thus, a new theory had come to mind: a kind of hypothesis in which a theory of the functioning of the mind and a theory of the functioning of the body were seen to be two ways of explaining a single situation. I was naturally excited by my new idea and anxious to find evidence to support or contradict it. I returned to my physiology books, tested my hypothesis against the current theories of medical science, and in the end could find no reason to doubt my theory. That was over twenty years ago. In the meantime, what I first felt to be a very tentative theory or hypothesis has become my belief. I believe, like Dr. Menninger, that the task of our life is to balance the opposing forces which are forever active in our minds *and* in our bodies; that the problem of balance in our lives can be viewed both psychologically and physiologically. Thus, to balance and harmonize the body is to balance and harmonize the mind. The differing observations and theories are simply two ways of looking at the same fundamental situation, the same fundamental problem. The fundamental problem is life itself. How to bring balance and harmony to our lives from moment to moment is the problem. How to live is the problem. To study Buddhism is to study how to live.

QUESTIONS AND ANSWERS

Sensei, when I studied the nervous system in my high school biology class, it did not seem particularly relevant to my life at the time. Now I can't remember a thing. I wonder if you could talk about the autonomic nervous system in more detail. Just how does it work?

Well, I'm not really qualified to explain the workings of the autonomic nervous system in terms of chemical reactions and so forth, but I think the broad pattern of its action can be understood without getting into such technical details. When we study the human body scientifically, we are always confronted by its wonderous complexity. Its parts, their functions, and their interactions can be understood in many ways. Nowadays, we generally understand the body as a complex of systems, each system fulfilling a particular need, a particular role in the life of the body. All of these systems are important, indeed vital, yet we are generally unaware of their functioning or even of their existence. They operate, for the most part, without our conscious control. In fact, most of the organs which are associated with these various systems are independently active; that is, they function spontaneously. Do you remember dissecting frogs in your biology class? Remember the heart? It continued beating even after being removed from the frog's body, didn't it? This is a nice example of the independent or autonomous action of the organs of the body. But the organs and systems of the body must work together if life is to be maintained. Each organ and system must fulfill its function in coordination with all the other organs and systems of the body. The organs and systems which we study separately in biology class are parts of a grand system which is the body itself. This larger system must work in a coordinated fashion, a harmonized fashion. A state of internal equilibrium or balance must be maintained. This balanced state cannot be a static state, however. The internal conditions of the body and the external conditions of the environment are constantly changing. Somehow then, the body must meet the particular demands of the moment, and at the same time maintain a state of over-all equilibrium and harmony. This is the task of the autonomic or involuntary nervous system. It takes its name from the fact that it, like the organs it regulates, is not ordinarily subject to our conscious control.

In regard to the ideas we have been discussing, the most interesting aspect of the autonomic nervous system is the mechanism by which it influences the activity of the various organs and systems of the body. As I mentioned earlier, the autonomic nervous system has two parts: the sympathetic and parasympathetic systems. The nerve fibers of the two systems travel in separate pathways to the organs of the body and their effects upon those organs are generally specific and antagonistic.

For example, when the sympathetic nerves are in a state of heightened activity, the heart beats faster and with stronger force. On the other hand, when parasympathetic activity increases, the heart beats more slowly. The two systems do not work alternately, however, but simultaneously. Thus, at any given time, the output of blood from the heart is dependent upon the relative strength of the two nerve systems at that moment.

The two sides of the autonomic nervous system have similarly contradictory effects upon the other systems of the body. Generally speaking, the sympathetic nervous system causes tensing, constricting, or excitation of the body's organs, while the parasympathetic system has a relaxing effect. As we have seen, the functioning of some organs, like the heart, is enhanced when the influence of the sympathetic nerves is stronger than that of the parasympathetic nerves. In other cases, however, the effect may be reversed. The stomach and digestive system, for example, tend to work harder when parasympathetic activity is stronger than sympathetic activity.

So perhaps you can begin to see how the autonomic nervous system regulates the internal conditions of the body. It seems to be a very intricately balanced system whereby the activity of particular organs is subtly influenced by continually adjusted levels of sympathetic and parasympathetic nervous activity.

You may wonder, then, just how the autonomic nervous system itself is regulated. We can consider this problem from both a general and a specific point of view. Generally speaking, the autonomic nervous system responds to changes in the internal and external environment. When our circumstances change, the autonomic nervous system reacts to those changes following certain set patterns of response. In the broadest sense, then, we can say that the autonomic nervous system is regulated by the conditions of our lives, by the totality of factors which make up our situation at a particular moment in time.

In a more specific sense, we can talk about the mechanism which brings about changes in the activity of the autonomic nervous system. The internal conditions of the body are monitored by nerve receptors which run from the organs to various control centers in the autonomic nervous system. So any change in the internal environment can trigger immediate action by the sympathetic or parasympathetic systems.

Sensory information from the external world also leads to changes in the activity of the autonomic nerves. This information is usually received and interpreted by the cortex, which is directly linked to a small structure in the brain called the hypothalamus. The hypothalamous is in turn linked to the nerves of the autonomic nervous system. This seems to suggest that the hypothalamous is the control center which initiates activity of the autonomic nerves in response to changes in the external environment.

This idea has been substantiated by medical researchers. They have found that, in its structure, the hypothalamous reflects the dual nature of the autonomic nervous system. It is composed of two lobes. Artificial stimulation of one lobe increases sympathetic nervous activity, while stimulation of the other lobe inhibits the same activity. This pattern has also been observed in studying the effects of dramatic changes in the external environment upon the hypothalamous and the autonomic nervous system. For example, when we are in a dangerous or stressful situation, impulses from the cortex reach the hypothalamous, which in turn initiates strong levels of sympathetic nervous activity. This brings about wide ranging effects in the body which enhance our readiness to deal with the emergency. These effects include increased metabolism, elevated blood pressure, increased heart action and blood flow to the muscles, and decreased blood flow to the digestive system. This is the so-called fight-or-flight response.

From this example, we can easily see the general tendency of increased sympathetic nervous activity. When the influence of the sympathetic nervous system is greater than that of the parasympathetic system, we are in a state of heightened mental and physical tension. We are, simply speaking, set to fight. We tend to be too aggressive, too excited, too positive and critical in our thinking. In extreme cases we may be prone to cruelty and violence. In other words, the state of heightened sympathetic nervous activity is analogous to the force of hate in Dr. Menninger's system. On the other hand, when parasympathetic nervous activity is stronger than sympathetic nervous activity, we tend to be too passive, too protective, and too sensual. We are prone to laziness, listlessness, and over-indulgence. This then corresponds to the other force in Dr. Menninger's theory, that is, love.

If all these ideas seem too abstract and theoretical, stop to think for a minute about times when you have faced difficult or tense situations. Did you sometimes find yourself making a hurried trip to the toilet? This is another effect of an unbalanced response of the autonomic nervous system. It may be humorous to think about in retrospect, but I think it points up an interesting fact. That is, that the condition of our autonomic nerves has very real and sometimes disturbing consequences in our day-to-day lives. It is one thing to observe, intellectually, that we cannot control the autonomic nervous system, but it is rather disquieting to realize that, in a very fundamental and real sense, the state of our autonomic nervous system determines our conduct in the world. When it comes right down to it, we can't even control the movement of our bowels!

This idea may take some getting used to. We are accustomed to thinking that we are in control of our lives; that by our thoughts and conscious decisions we can determine our actions and situation in the world. We feel that we can or should be able to solve the problems of life intellectually. But when we realize that a system over which we have almost no conscious control actually determines the most important aspects of our life, then we may begin to have a different outlook on life itself. We may begin to see that our life, our conduct, and even our destiny are not problems of mind alone; but of body and mind. We may then realize that we have been working on our problems in a one-sided fashion. What we need is a method of working on the state of our body and mind as a whole. What we need is a method of promoting the equilibrium of the autonomic nervous system.

I often find myself resisting theories, such as yours, which attempt to explain human life or behavior on the basis of physical science. They always seem too mechanistic, too limited in scope. Surely life is more than flesh and bones...

Yes, I can understand your feelings, but please think about this lecture within the context of our previous discussions. We have been talking about viewpoints, about various ways of seeing and interpreting the world. My aim has been, first of all, to point out the fact that we do indeed see the world differently from different standpoints, and secondly, to provide some theoretical explanations for that fact. But I think it is impossible to explain our situation with a single theory. Dr. Menninger's theory seems to me a good way to explain the mental or psychological side of our situation, but we should not ignore the other side of that situation, the physical side. The physical or material side of our existence is surely just as important as the mental or spiritual side. But when we look at the physical side of life, we cannot explain it in terms of psychological or mental theories. The body must be explained in physical terms: in terms of muscles, bones, blood, nerves and so forth. So I feel that my explanation of our situation in terms of the autonomic nervous system is a valid explanation. I think it is an important interpretation of life as seen from the physical side.

On the other hand, I would not like to suggest that my theory is the only way to explain the situation of our physical existence on this earth. There are many ways. There are many standpoints. I would only hope that by expressing my ideas, sincere scientists might be moved to consider the problem further—to explore the meaning of this life, again and again.

Do you really think that life can be explained?

There is always some factor in life which cannot be explained.
From the ultimate standpoint, life, the universe, and reality
itself are ineffable. But I would not like to hide behind this
screen of mystery. Ultimately, reality may indeed be ineffable,
but the various modes of perceiving and understanding reality
can be defined, and the relationships between them illuminated.
This is, I think, the value of Buddhist philosophy. Buddhist
theory contains a very exact system of thought, a kind of
logic. By using that logic, I think we can learn much about the
structure of human thought and the ways we organize our perceptions of the world. There are many things about life and
about Buddhism itself which can be understood.

Many priests do not affirm my opinion. They say that Buddhism
cannot be explained. They speak about life in vague and mystical terms. Such explanations may, at times, be inspiring, but
they rarely tell us very much about our real situation. We are
living in the modern world. It is a rational world, a logical
world. It demands rational explanations, logical explanations.
This is why I try to explain Buddhist theory and the fundamental situation of our life in scientific terms. I think our
situation demands such an effort. So, to answer your question,
I must say yes and no. Life can be explained, and at the same
time it is ineffable. That is our situation.

IDEALISM AND MATERIALISM

Now I would like to try to bring together some of the ideas we have been discussing. In the preceeding chapters, I attempted to point out some of the characteristics of our world; that is, the world as we usually see it, experience it, and understand it. The picture which emerges from such a study is one of division, disunity and conflict. At the simplest level of understanding, we find the existence of two worlds: the worlds of thinking and feeling. We have a tendency to divide what we think—our ideas—from what we feel or sense—the external world. Our recognition of the two worlds or realms is usually not so clear, but a vague awareness does exist and this awareness provides a basis for organizing our perceptions and thoughts. The discriminating functions of the intellect serve to define and support such a divided view of life. We make sense of our world, first by breaking it into parts, then by classifying, rearranging and comparing those parts in our minds. In the process, certain polar opposites appear which become the foundations of our common-sense understanding of life. The very basic conceptions of mind and body, man and nature, which we discussed in some detail, are only two of the many dualistic interpretations which form the substance of our thoughts. Complicating the situation still more, we find that in the very core of our beings there exists a system of intricate balance and sensitivity—a system which works to stabilize and harmonize our lives, but which can, if tilted off-center, push us toward the extremes of aggression and hate on one side, and passivity and dependent love on the other.

So it seems that we are living in a very complicated world, a chaotic world. I think the word *chaos* is an apt description of our situation. In our lives we are constantly pushed and pulled by the conflicting ideas, perceptions and emotions which confront each other in our consciousness. We see one side of life and then the other, but we cannot find the middle ground, the middle way. In the confusion of our daily lives we often seem to lose our bearings, our sense of balance. We don't know which way to turn or what to do. It is very painful. Indeed, there are times when pain and suffering seem the only constant factors in our lives. Living in chaos is not so easy.

I think it is important to recognize the chaotic quality of our lives and of the world in which we live. My purpose in the preceeding chapters was to paint a kind of picture of that chaotic world. But painting such a picture may be a problem in itself. Looking at our problems one by one tends to obscure the fact that some underlying pattern does exist in the midst of those problems. So now I would like to turn your attention to that underlying pattern. For me, that pattern emerges most clearly when I consider the historical origins of our world. I believe that in studying those origins we can find the fundamental basis of chaos itself; and if we can understand that fundamental basis, I believe we can have some hope of finding the way out of chaos and into a new world—a world of peace and harmony.

The study of history always invites a variety of interpretations. My personal interpretation of history flows naturally from my understanding of life as a Buddhist. For this reason, my conclusions may seem a bit startling or irritating to those whose ideas and attitudes have been nurtured and molded in more traditional disciplines. Unfortunately, there is little space here to present a convincing argument in support of my ideas. I can only offer a brief outline of my understanding and hope that the ideas contained therein will spark some interest and debate among those who study history as a profession. I believe that such a debate would be of great benefit to the modern world. I think that from such a debate a new understanding of the origins of our situation would emerge, and with that new understanding would come fresh hope of resolving the great conflicts at the heart of this confusing and chaotic world.

In thinking about the origins of Western civilization, I usually look to the ancient Greeks as my starting point. Greek civilization at its peak was rich, complex, and beautiful. Its economy was based on a kind of slavery, so in addition to their wealth, the citizens of Greece enjoyed an even more precious commodity: time. They had time to play, time to study, time to enjoy art and the beauty of nature. They had time to think. In less fortunate societies, thinking was valued only for its practical applications to the problem of survival; but in Greece, thinking came to be valued for its own sake. Those who thought most deeply and expressed their thoughts most clearly and beautifully were honored and esteemed. They were the philosophers.

Among the Greek philosophers was one called Plato. In him, the Greek reverence for thinking came to a kind of culmination. For Plato believed that the world of thinking was the real world itself. In his life, he came to distrust the reality of the world revealed by his senses. To him, it was a fickle world, a world of ever-changing appearances about which no true knowledge was possible. But while he could doubt the reality of his sensory perceptions, he could not doubt the reality of his own thinking; and the ideas which appeared and evolved in his consciousness were to him much more real and substantial than the fleeting perceptions of the external world. So he came to believe in the existence of a world other than this world. It was a perfect world, a world of eternal Forms or Ideas. These archetypal Forms could not be perceived by the senses, but through a kind of direct mental contact which could be realized in contemplation. Such contemplation, Plato believed, was the source of all true knowledge, and he devoted his entire life to its practice. For such contemplation, Plato esteemed the value of mathematics very highly. He believed that the exact relations among numbers revealed the underlying plan or structure of the world of Forms and that, by studying such relations, the inner harmony of that world could be seen and personally realized.

When I was young, it was very difficult for me to appreciate the value of Platonic philosophy. To me, Plato's belief that the real world was not this world but a world of ideas was very hard to swallow. It seemed to fly in the face of common sense. I could not believe that ideas were real and the evidence of my senses a kind of illusion. But later in my life, I came to realize that Plato's thought was one of the most important foundations of Western civilization. His philosophical theories were the source of the great stream of Western thought known as idealism. In the centuries since Plato lived, idealistic philosophy has varied greatly in its forms, but the spirit of Plato's thought is always clearly evident. That spirit can be seen not only in the theoretical systems of idealistic philosophers, but in the fundamental character of Western civilization itself. For even though Plato's notion of a world of Forms seems incredible from the standpoint of common sense, we must recognize that the fundamental basis of his philosophy was an almost perfect reverence for the human intellect; and that reverence of the intellect and the ideas it produces has been, and continues to be, one of the most remarkable characteristics of Western civilization. I believe then that Plato's philosophy was of tremendous importance, not only in the realm of ideas, but in the shaping of every other aspect of our society. Even the material and technological advances of Western civilization owe much to the man who saw in mathematics the key to the world of Ideas. Without a great reverence for mathematics, could we have ever reached the moon?

Between Plato and the Apollo rocket there was, of course, a

long gap of time. Plato's understanding of the world was inherited and modified by his greatest student, Aristotle. In his thinking, Aristotle moved away from many of his teacher's positions, especially in relation to the theory of Forms. Thus, his philosophy was not so purely idealistic as Plato's, but in his writings we find that Aristotle did retain his teacher's reverence for the intellect as the basis of all true knowledge. His own theories were a splendid testament to the ability of the human mind to construct a coherent and meaningful philosophical system. That system of thought, along with Platonic philosophy and Greek philosophy in general, spread to the Roman Empire and there met with Christianity.

The meeting of a young idealistic religion from the Near East with the idealistic philosophy of Greece was an event of profound importance in the evolution of Western civilization. In the theories of the two greatest Greek philosophers, the Christian theologians found a very excellent and compatible theoretical system on which to base their own idealistic beliefs. The mixing of Christian and Greek idealism produced a new and powerful thought which was to rule over Western society until the end of the Middle Ages. Among the Christian theologians who worked, first to reconcile the teachings of the Bible with Greek philosophy, and then to explain and propagate this new thought, were Saint Augustine(354-430) and Thomas Aquinas (1224-74). These two were very excellent philosophers in their own rights, and their thought contributed greatly to the strength and vitality of Christianity. I usually think of the period bounded by these two theologians as the age of Western idealism.

A more graphic and popular name for that period is the Dark Ages, and for most people it must have been a truly dark and dismal time. Living conditions were harsh and depressing. The feudal economy, based on primitive methods of agricultural production, was dependent on the hard physical labor of peasants who made up the majority of the population. These peasants were bound to a lord throughout their lives, a lord who took his authority directly from God. Thus the Church assumed a prominent role in maintaining the peaceful order of society. Since there could be little hope of achieving happiness on this earth, the people were urged to look forward to a new and happy life in heaven.

Such a happy existence was not given freely: it had to be earned through sacrifice and obedience to the laws of God and the teachings of the religious authorities who interpreted those laws. The aim of life was thus to prepare the spirit for its life in the next world. In this endeavor the pains, pleasures, and desires of physical existence could only be regarded as hindrances or obstacles to the goal. To realize that goal it was, in fact, necessary to deny the body altogether. In a life of almost continual labor, such denial was not so difficult as it might sound. Pain and physical suffering were either ignored or stoically endured. Desire, often muted by the simple fact of physical exhaustion, was suppressed. And the physical pleasures of the body were seen as sins to be overcome through repentance and religious fervor. The religious fervor came naturally from the tension caused by the denial of the body and the physical realm. To live as human beings, people must recognize both the physical and spiritual sides of their existence, but in the days when idealistic thought ruled the Western world, such a balanced life was quite impossible. People's emotions often drifted between despair and supressed anger. Life was very grim. To look to heaven for deliverance was the only real hope.

The time came, however, when people began to throw off their Medieval yokes. The revival of art and literature in the 14th, 15th, and 16th centuries is usually called the Renaissance. It is said that the Renaissance began in Italy and that one of the primary catalysts for the change was the wealth which accumulated there as a result of trade with the Orient. The generally affluent conditions gradually released people from the economic and spiritual domination of the Church and the feudal landlords. They began to live as human beings, that is, as men and women who had their own minds *and* bodies. This was, I believe, a very important change, a fundamental change in the way people perceived themselves and the world. I think the recognition of the physical side of life in the Renaissance was the dawn of a new age in Western civilization: the age of modern materialism.

This change in the fundamental perceptions of people was reflected by changes within the Church, as well as in secular society. In the early part of the 16th century, Martin Luther (1483-1546) and John Calvin(1509-64) led a movement which I interpret as an effort to change the Christianity of God into the Christianity of human beings. The Reformation is thus seen by some as a deterioration of Christianity and the authority of the Church, but I believe it should be esteemed as the time when Christians began to live as human beings for the first time.

A similar interpretation sheds light on the meaning of political movements which had their inception in that era and culminated some two hundred years later in the American and French Revolutions. In the Middle Ages, people had generally believed that the right of kings to rule came from God. But, in the new intellectual climate of the 16th and 17th centuries, men began to question the divine right of kings; they began to realize that ordinary people could govern their own countries; that countries should in fact belong to the people: They had begun to wake up from their long Medieval dream of the spirit to find the bright potentialities of life in this physical universe.

Nowhere was the new intellectual climate more evident than in England. There, thinkers like Francis Bacon(1561-1626), Thomas Hobbes(1581-1679), John Locke(1632-1702), George Berkeley(1685-1753), and David Hume(1711-76) were laying the foundations of modern materialistic thought. These men found it very difficult to believe in the spiritual thinking of most idealistic philosophers. They challenged the idea that knowledge could come from pure thinking or contemplation. For them, empirical evidence was the only reliable teacher; therefore the role of the senses became of primary importance. If they could not confirm an idea or theory with the evidence of their senses, they were reluctant to concede its reality or truth. In thus shifting the focus of attention away from the world of ideas and toward the external world as perceived by the senses, these empiricist philosophers were changing the foundation on which the understanding of life and the world was based. In so doing, they revealed the existence of a new world. This was the orderly world of matter, form, and energy. It was an intriguing world, a world to be explored and explained by scientific observation and experimentation. The world of modern materialism had been born.

Of course, not all philosophers embraced this new viewpoint. Many continued to follow the stream of idealistic thought which had been ingrained in the thinking of Western society for so long. These modern idealistic thinkers were led by the French philosopher, René Descartes, who established his philosophy on the basis of the famous words, "Cogito ergo sum" or "I think, therefore I am." These words show that the focus of his theory was on the mind or the subject which thinks, and such a focus is the primary characteristic of all idealistic thought. Descartes is usually considered to be a philosopher of both mind and matter, so we should not call him a pure idealist, but at the same time, we must acknowledge the fundamentally idealistic slant of his thinking.

At this point the existence of two sharply divergent streams of thought became apparent. On one side, there were the materialistic theories of the English empiricists; on the other, the idealistic theories of the Continental philosophers. This clear-cut division continued until the German philosopher, Immanuel Kant(1724-1804), attempted to combine or synthesize the two streams of thought into one grand system based on his theory of reason. His successors, however, did not maintain his balanced viewpoint and, instead, returned to the idealistic stream of thought. Their efforts culminated in the philosophy of George Hegel(1770-1831) who carried the idealistic interpretation of the world to an almost perfect conclusion. In his splendid theory of spiritual phenomenology, the whole universe is seen and explained as manifestations of the 'World Spirit'. In attempting to explain all things from only one standpoint, Hegel created a theory of great, but flawed beauty. For such an extreme viewpoint always contains the potential for being converted into its polar opposite. This is in fact what happened.

Among Hegel's follower's were some who considered their teacher's standpoint to be too idealistic. These students split away from the main stream of Hegelian thought and, out of this left leaning school, a new theory emerged which turned Hegel's system completely upside down. Karl Marx discovered that, by replacing his teacher's 'World Spirit' with matter, he could explain the whole of existence in an utterly new way.

Marx's new theory was profoundly disturbing to the European people. They realized that, if it were possible to explain all phenomena on the basis of matter, there could be no place for Christianity to exist. Such a heightened awareness of the irreconcilable differences between two systems of thought produced a situation in which the differences among people were exposed and highly exaggerated. In such a polarized situation, actual conflict was almost inevitable. And so it was that in the latter half of the 19th century, Western civilization fell into a chaotic confusion of societies in which every aspect of life came to reflect the conflict in the mind and body of man; that is, the conflict between idealism and materialism.

This then is our heritage and our fundamental situation. We are caught in a world divided, a world in which conflict and confrontation appear inevitable, and compromise serves only to postpone the day of final reckoning. In such a world it is difficult to feel optimistic about the future, but I think there are in fact some reasons for hope. One is that the very clarity of the conflict between idealism and materialism has stimulated the search for a resolution to the conflict. Since the middle of the 19th century, many philosophers have been engaged in such a search. Notable among them are the so-called existentialist philosophers: men like Kierkegaard(1813-1855), Jaspers(1883-1969), Heidegger(1889-   ), and Sartre(1905-1980). Their theories are quite varied, so among them it is difficult to find a common ground, but it appears to me that they have all made efforts to resolve the conflict between idealism and materialism. Their thought is yet very young and immature, but I think their theories are very important. I think that they contain the seeds of eventual liberation from the chaos of modern life.

You may be wondering how philosophical theories could change the world; in fact, they cannot. Theory alone cannot save us. By themselves, philosophies have little power to influence events in the real world. But the line between philosophy and religion is a fine and tenuous one. Every philosophy is a religion in embryo, a religion in search of believers. When a philosophy becomes a religion it gains the power of religion: the power to influence men's actions, the power to change the world.

So theory alone cannot save us; but if a philosophy which resolved the fundamental conflict between idealism and materialism could meet and shake hands with a religion which had the same theoretical basis, then the situation might be greatly changed. This is my small hope for the future of mankind. I believe that in the not-too-distant future, Western civilization will find the theory and practice it needs to heal the divisions in its collective heart and mind. I believe that it will find that theory and practice in Buddhism, and I believe that when Western civilization and Buddhism join hands, human beings will find the life of peace and harmony which has been their dream for thousands of years.

QUESTIONS & ANSWERS

Your historical analysis of the development of Western thought is interesting, but I always have trouble relating such explanations to my own personal life. They always seem irrelevant somehow...

Historical analysis is always objective in nature and this objective character often gives such studies an impersonal feeling, but we should not suppose that the history of human thought and action is therefore irrelevant to our lives today. We are what we are precisely because of that history. The intellectual viewpoints of idealism and materialism are not simply abstract theories in books. They exist in each and every one of us. We absorb the intellectual, religious, and social attitudes and habits of our parents and friends, just as they received their fundamental outlooks from their parents and their parents' parents. We have thus inherited a tremendous legacy from the past, a legacy with many confusing and contradictory elements.

At times in our lives we may have perfect faith in the idealistic teachings of a traditional religion. At other times those beliefs may appear silly and outdated. Then we are prone to believe in the natural superiority of objective research and analysis. We admire the arts and sciences which have progressed so much since the time of the Renaissance and the French Revolution. But as we move from one intellectual standpoint to another, we cannot avoid some feelings of doubt. We cannot help wondering if our interpretation of life is really true. Thus we find that the historical conflict between idealism and materialism is precisely our problem. The conflicting ways of seeing and interpreting the world, which have evolved over many centuries, are precisely the conflicts and turmoil in our own bodies and minds.

So, if you find the historical analysis of our situation too impersonal, it might be well for you to consider the qualities of your own outlook or bias. We often reveal the way we look at the world by the kind of questions we ask, and by the kind of problems we find in our lives. For some of us, the most important problems in life are mental in nature. They are problems of ideas or problems of mind. They may be religious, ethical, or psychological problems, but in spite of their variety, they all seem to share a certain subjective quality: the relation-ship between the problems and ourselves as subjects is always of paramount importance.

Others among us tend to find the real problems of life in the external world. These problems revolve around things, money, comfort, and sensual gratification. Such problems are seen objectively. They have an impersonal or realistic quality.

So it seems that we can find two kinds of problems in our lives: problems of mind and problems of body. We may recognize and struggle with both types of problems, but, generally speak-ing, we feel that one type of problem is more important than the other, that one type of problem is the real root of all our problems.

Our problems are the focal point of our lives. They receive our attention and concern. It seems natural, then, that if we perceive our problems as having a particular source, we will believe that source to be the most fundamental basis of life itself. If our problems appear to arise in the mind, we will naturally believe in the importance of mind and the reality of thought. If, on the other hand, we feel that our problems arise in the external world, then we will believe that the external world is the only reality.

And so our personal interpretations of life—our world-views—eventually take on a certain orientation or slant. We tend to see all things from a certain side, from a certain point of view. Our thoughts run in certain familiar patterns or grooves, and we cannot see or accept the existence of anything which does not fall within the limits of our vision. This is the meaning and the origin of bias and prejudice. It is the origin of conflicts and wars. The conflict between idealism and materialism is very real. It is never irrelevant to our lives, here and now.

So it seems that if a person has a materialistic or idealistic outlook, it will affect his whole life. Is this true? Could you say something about the practical effects of our philosophical orientations?

Idealists tend to spend a lot of time in the library. Perhaps that sounds funny, but I think it is a common characteristic of people who have an idealistic orientation toward life. They believe in ideas, so they search for ideas in every place and in every situation. Their search takes them in many directions, but it often leads them to become interested in religion or philosophy. Their readings in these areas usually reinforce their natural belief in the importance of mind. This belief may cause them to be contemptuous of life in this world. They dream of a better world, an ideal world.

Since idealists are convinced of the reality of their ideas and ideals, they are usually quite diligent in their efforts to realize them. They are often quite fearless—willing to risk anything for their god, philosophical system, or ideal world. Actual facts, real problems are just nuisances to be brushed aside or ignored. Idealists are thus blind to anything which does not fit the pattern of their thought. They march resolutely ahead, only to stumble again and again on the hard rocks of reality.

Materialists, on the other hand, are forever on the lookout for those rocks. They are fascinated by the beauty of some, the texture or hardness of others, and they would like to avoid the sharp and dangerous rocks at all costs. So materialists are usually engaged in a study of their situation in the external world. Their studies tend to be very exact and scientific. They collect data, analyze it carefully, and formulate theories based on their observations. This trait points up the close relationship between science and materialism. Science is very precise and methodical. Its interpretations of the world are very useful. But science can only study phenomena which has already occurred. It is rooted in the past. So, while it can provide excellent interpretations of past facts, it can't guide our actions at the moment of the present or in the future. But materialists are generally unaware of this. They try to model their lives according to their experiences in the past. They tend to be conservative. They are unwilling to try new things, preferring the safe and secure paths which worked well in the past. They are proud of their common sense and quick to criticize others whose ideas and behavior do not conform to their standards of rationality.

So we can say that materialists make excellent scientists and social commentators, but they cannot be the leaders of societies. To be a leader one must have the courage to try new things, to think new thoughts, to act. Materialists dislike action, dislike change and new ideas, dislike anything which might threaten their security. They are in love with the sensuous aspects of life, but it is difficult for them to live spontaneously in the moment of the present. They are always trying to recreate a comfortable situation from the past.

In your explanation of the origins of idealistic and materialistic philosophy, you find a clear link between those two intellectual viewpoints and the worlds of thinking and feeling. In an earlier lecture you said that, from the Buddhist standpoint, our perceptions or interpretation of reality as a world of thinking or a world of feeling was a kind of delusion. Do you believe, then, that both idealistic and materialistic philosophy are based on delusions or misconceptions about the nature of reality?

Yes, I do. This is a very important point. Human beings create their philosophies on the basis of their delusions. This is a fact. In the history of Western civilization there was a very great delusion—a fundamental delusion. That is idealism. Greek and Christian idealistic thought were of tremendous importance in molding the fundamental character of Western civilization.

IDEALISM AND MATERIALISM

That fundamental character is its intellectualism or its tendency to interpret all things on the basis of dualistic thought. This tendency led naturally and inevitably to the emergence of another philosophy, a system of thought with an entirely different standpoint or basis, that is materialism. The competition between these two divergent streams of thought produced our world, our civilization. It is a truly great civilization—a civilization of splendid beauty, diversity, and vitality. So when we look at the historical process which has produced our world, we must recognize the importance of intellectualism and the value of the delusions on which it is based. Without those delusions, there could be no history. This is a rather startling conclusion, but it is true, I think. Plato had absolute faith in the existence of a world of perfect Forms or Ideas. This was his delusion, his misconception about the nature of reality—and it is out of such delusions that our world has evolved.

So I think we should esteem the intellectual theories and philosophies which have been so important in the evolution of our world, but at the same time we should recognize that the two opposing streams of Western thought have reached a kind of impasse or deadlock. This is our situation today. So we are faced with a difficult challenge; that is, to find a way past the deadlock, to find a solution to the conflict between idealism and materialism. Such a solution cannot be found by denying one thought or the other. That has been tried many times in the past. Only on the basis of a sincere appreciation of both tendencies in Western thought can we have a reasonable hope of finding a new religion or philosophy on which to build our lives. This is my belief.

Your vision of the future is inspiring, but your insistence on the importance or value of Western thought is surprising to me. When I look at the world today, it appears to me that Western society has actually forsaken idealism altogether. The old idealistic religions have become almost powerless in the rush toward materialistic gain. To me it seems that the merit of

TO MEET THE REAL DRAGON

*Buddhism and other Oriental religions is that they can teach us
a rationale for returning to a more spiritual or harmonious way
of life. What do you think?*

I cannot dispute your observations about the materialistic
character of modern Western society. Western society today is
materialistic. However, I feel that there is some danger in
your idea of "returning" to a more spiritual way of life. Of
course a peaceful and harmonious life is something we can all
hope for, something we can all strive to attain, but is such a
life to be found through a rejection of material culture, a
return to the spiritual purity of an earlier age?

I don't think so. Western civilization has had its spiritual
age, its age of idealism. For many people that was not an
especially happy or harmonious time in which to live. They had
no freedom to act, no freedom to know or enjoy the physical
side of life. Every aspect of life was bound by the rigid ideas
and attitudes of an idealistic religion and society. The Renaissance, the Reformation, and the French Revolution were all
efforts to throw off the shackles of an idealistic vision of
the universe.

Such efforts continued for a long time. They continue today. As
a result, we have gone to the other extreme. We find ourselves
living in a rather hedonistic society; a society in which
morality, ethics, and religious beliefs are increasingly under
attack; a society in which the value of all things is computed
in dollars, yen, or rubles. Such a society is not difficult to
criticize. It should be criticized.

But in our rush to criticize the materialism of modern society,
we have a tendency to forget the lessons of history. We fail to
see that our situation has evolved through a long process—a
process that is continuing today. Many would like to reverse
the process. They would like to go back to a more primitive and
natural way of life. They would like to return to an age of
simple hopes and simple ideas. It is an appealing notion, a

rather romantic idea, but I'm afraid it is an impossible dream.

We cannot reverse the flow of history. We cannot negate the lives of those who came before. We have come to this point in time on the backs of our ancestors. We should not deny the value of their lives. We should not reject their contributions to the world. This is why I esteem the value of Western thought. Throughout the long history of Western civilization, people have been searching for the common basis of human society. I esteem this effort. I believe that this effort has brought us to the neighborhood of a new civilization. In this new civilization the excesses of the age of idealism and the age of materialism will be overcome. Society will transcend spiritual culture and material culture and in their place a new and truly human society will emerge. I hope and believe that Buddhism will play an important role in the emergence of this new society, this new civilization of human beings.

GAUTAMA BUDDHA

This is a book about Buddhism. In some of the preceeding chapters the exact relationship between Buddhism and the topics under discussion must have seemed rather obscure. We have looked at various facets of human thinking and feeling, the ways we see and understand the world, the forces at work in the body and mind, the evolution of human thought and civilization. In short, we have been studying human life and understanding in its various aspects and forms. We have been studying human beings and the meaning of being human. This is in fact what it means to study Buddhism. Buddhism is Humanism. It is a thoroughly human religion, a religion which exalts the dignity of human beings as they actually are.

So if we are to understand Buddhism we must understand what it means to be human. This was my purpose in exploring the various topics in the first part of this book. I hoped to establish a kind of base or foundation on which to build an understanding of human life, for such a theoretical understanding is also a prerequisite for the understanding of Buddhism itself. Now I think we are ready to begin a more direct investigation of this human religion called Buddhism. The most natural starting point is Gautama Buddha himself. He was the source, the origin, the spring from which the Buddhist religion arose. The story of Gautama Buddha's life is well known to most Buddhists and to many non-Buddhists as well. It has been told again and again, and rightfully so, for it is out of his experience of life that his peculiar understanding of life arose. It stands to reason, then, that if we can gain some understanding of the important circumstances, events, and experiences which contributed to Gautama Buddha's understanding of life, we should also gain some important insights into the meaning of Buddhism itself. So I would like to tell the story of Gautama Buddha's life once more. I would like to tell the story in my own way, according to my own understanding.

About 2,500 years ago there was a small kingdom in the southern foothills of the Himalayas which was known as the land of the Sakayas. One day the king of the Sakayas was informed that his wife had just given birth to a baby boy. Following tradition, the king called for his spiritual advisor, a Brahman priest, to come and bless his new son and heir. When the priest saw the boy, he sensed that there was something special in the boy's appearance. He was moved to make a prediction concerning the boy's future. The king's son, he said, had great promise. He was destined to become a leader of men. That leadership might evolve in one of two directions. Either the boy would extend his talent in the area of political power, or he would turn to more spiritual or philosophical pursuits. If he followed the first path, he would become the ruler of all India. If the second path were chosen, he would probe the depths of human understanding. He would find a new truth and become a teacher of men.

For the king, the prophesy was at once hopeful and disturbing. He was a proud and practical man. He wanted his son to retain and extend the power which he then enjoyed. But he knew that if his son became involved with religion and philosophy he would lose all interest in secular life. How, he wondered, could he prevent such an unfortunate state of affairs from developing. He finally settled on a rather simple plan: He would protect his son from the darker side of life. By doing so, he hoped that his son's natural inquisitiveness would not be drawn to the inexplicable contradictions in the world; that he would not be troubled by moral doubt or philosophical conflict.

And so the king endeavored to make his son's life as happy and as free from care and conflict as possible. He surrounded him with beauty, comfort, and luxury. He gave strict orders concerning his education, and took special care that his son's world contained no hints of ugliness, decay, or death. Gautama Buddha's early world was thus a very special place. It was a kind of wonderland: a place where the young prince could wander freely among his toys and his daydreams, safely sheltered from the harsh realities just outside the palace walls.

In creating such an artificial world, the king inadvertently encouraged in his son the development of the philosophical sensitivities which he had hoped to suppress. Young Gautama Buddha was often moved by seemingly insignificant events. One day as he watched a farmer working in a field, the farmer's plow cut through an earthworm and left it wriggling and twitching helplessly on the surface of the soil. Suddenly a bird swooped down and carried the still struggling worm away. The boy watching the scene felt a stabbing pain of sadness and pity in his heart. He saw at that moment that all living beings must kill in order to survive. That knowledge cast a shadow on his pretty world. He began to look at things more closely, to wonder what dark secrets they might conceal. He became especially curious about the world outside the palace walls, and the day came when those wall could no longer contain the young prince.

The scriptures report that he went first to the east gate. There he saw a very old man. His body was bent and frail, his eyes sunken, his skin wrinkled and dark. The young prince had never seen such an ugly human being before. He was shocked and frightened. Retreating to the safety of the palace, he went on to the south gate. There, on the ground outside the gate, he found a man who was sick and suffering from disease. He was crippled and could not walk. With a growing feeling of pain and desperation, Gautama Buddha returned again to the palace and proceeded to the west gate. There he saw a group of people carrying something on their shoulders. Looking closer he saw that it was a body, a dead body being carried to a funeral pyre. The scene filled him with dread and the certain knowledge that all living beings must eventually die. At last he went to the north gate of the palace and there he met a man who was quite different from anyone he had seen before. His posture was straight and dignified. He wore simple, clean clothes, and his face appeared calm and peaceful as he walked quietly on his way. Though the prince had never seen such a man before, he knew that he was a sage or a *yogi*: a man who had renounced his social ties to live a life of quiet contemplation, a life in pursuit of the Truth. He found himself strangely attracted to the man, and the image of his peaceful face stayed with him for a long time.

Gautama Buddha's world was thus no longer the happy and beautiful world of his childhood. It had been invaded by a host of confusing facts and contradictory images. He found that he could no longer take comfort in simple ideas or pleasant daydreams. There were too many doubts and uncertainties. And it seemed that the more he learned about the realities of living in the world, the more his doubts and uncertainties increased. He had found a new, hard, and disturbing face of reality, and that face did not conform at all to the neat and tidy ideas of his early life.

Many of those ideas had come from the palace priests who had been in charge of his education. From them he had learned the fundamental beliefs and attitudes of Brahmanism. Those beliefs included faith in a creator, a god called Brahma, whose spirit was believed to be present in human beings in the form of an immaterial essence called Atman. According to Brahman theory, Atman was essentially identical to Brahma, and was thus to be revered as the link between man and god the creator. It was believed possible through prayer, meditation, and ritual purification to make Atman manifest in the mind and thus to achieve unity with the universal Atman or Brahma. According to Brahmanism, this was, in fact, the true aim of human life. Such an outlook naturally regarded the body and other aspects of physical existence to be of only secondary importance. The harsh realities of life, which had begun to trouble the young prince so much, were of little interest to the Brahman priests. Such facts were merely the trivial and tedious appearances of a transient phase in the life of the eternal spirit. Compared to the world of Brahma, they were only *maya*: a dream or illusion.

If this viewpoint had been the only one encountered by Gautama Buddha, he might have put aside his doubts and accepted the role which fate seemed to have ordained for him. But, while Brahmanism was the dominant religion, it was not the only philosophy competing in the arena of Indian society at that time. Many thinkers, scholars, and philosophers had begun to challenge the conventional wisdom of Brahmanism. Some were skeptics or agnostics who believed that nothing was knowable; that the real existence of all phenomena, all experience, and all thought was questionable, and that nothing, therefore, could be stated with certainty. Doubt was the only intelligent viewpoint, for it alone could not be assailed.

Other thinkers challenged Brahmanism by postulating their own systems which were based on a kind of radical naturalism, a belief that the raw and simple face of nature was the only reality. Following such beliefs, they maintained that spiritual philosophies, like Brahmanism, and the social values associated with them, were without any basis in reality. Morality and and ethics could thus be ignored, and the real order of the universe allowed to take its natural course. One of these philosophers carried this materialistic view to the ultimate extreme, declaring that to kill a person with a sword should not be viewed as an unethical act, for the facts were simple and clear: a thin plate of metal passes through some cells of a human body—nothing more, nothing less. To see the truth of this position was only a matter of observation. With such words, he challenged the Brahman priests to show him the source of their own beliefs.

TO MEET THE REAL DRAGON

In the viewpoints of the Brahman priests and their critics, we can easily see the underlying conflict between idealism and materialism. The conflict, as we have discussed before, is inherent in human beings. Thus, it is an age old conflict, a timeless conflict. In the history of mankind it has surfaced again and again, sometimes clearly and dramatically, sometimes obscured by the social and economic conditions of the time. The Indian society of Gautama Buddha's day was rather open and tolerant. The intellectual climate was free and vigorous. In such an atmosphere, it was quite natural for the inherent division in the way men see and understand the world to be exposed and strenuously debated.

I feel sure that young Gautama Buddha was well aware of the debates and the issues involved. For him, they were more than interesting intellectual problems, however. For him, they were real problems. The conflict between idealism and materialism was one he experienced very profoundly in his personal life. In his youth he had discovered the attraction of ideas, the wonder of understanding the world with the mind, and the rather bitter disappointment of finding the gap between the ideal and real life.

Later, as he entered manhood, he discovered new aspects of life. He found the pleasures of love and sensual contact, the pride of ownership, the mixed blessings and burdens of family life. It was a new world for him—a world to be seen, touched, and tasted fully. In his position of power and wealth he was free to explore that world, to experiment and indulge his passions and desires. Perhaps because of his freedom, he rather quickly found the limits of this new world. He found that pleasant activities often have unpleasant results. He discovered a certain heaviness or dullness in the world of things and possessions. The pursuit of sensual gratification became a boring and repetitive exercise. He found that his life had veered sharply away from the sincerity of his youth, and he felt the loss of his former ideals very keenly. Still, the material world had a certain substantiality. It seemed real.

GAUTAMA BUDDHA

What was real? Where did the truth lie?

The debates between the priests and the materialistic thinkers clarified the questions in Gautama Buddha's mind, but they did not provide any convincing answers. Theoretical arguments only seemed to increase his confusion. He yearned for a fundamental Truth, a Truth which could bring real contentment and peace, as opposed to intellectual theories which always seemed to raise more doubts than they resolved. So he began to search for a new approach to his problems. He became interested in the teachings of the *yogis*, those mysterious holy men who sought spiritual liberation in a life free from the ties of secular society. Their thought had much in common with the philosophical beliefs of Brahmanism, but they rejected simple prayer and ritual as the means of attaining union with the absolute. They insisted that in order to attain the Truth it was necessary to undergo some arduous training—to embark on a path of spiritual hard work and discipline. Such a path became increasingly attractive to the young prince. At the age of twenty-nine, he resolved to leave his confused and petty world, find a master, and seek the meaning of his life.

He went first to the city of Vaisali and there met a teacher named Arada Kalama. Master Kalama claimed to have found a way to perfect freedom: the freedom of a man who wants nothing—the freedom of a state without desire. Attaining such a state was a matter of learning and practicing certain meditative techniques. So Gautama Buddha joined Master Kalama's order, and within a short time mastered the techniques which his teacher recommended. He found that he could indeed enter a state which was free from desire, but he also found that the state was a transient one: that soon after he finished his practice, his normal thoughts and feelings came flooding back, leaving him more confused and frustrated than before.

So he left the Master and wandered south to Magadha. There he met Master Ramaputra. This master promised to show him a deeper level of meditative absorption, a state transcending thinking and non-thinking. With renewed hope and energy the former prince learned the methods and teachings of his new master. He attained the state beyond thinking and non-thinking, but here again he found that the state was temporary and that it left him with no clearer understanding of the conflicts and problems which had compelled him to leave his home and begin his quest for the Truth.

Finally, he concluded that to attain the Truth he must conquer the confusion within himself without reliance on anything or anyone. He left Master Ramaputra and joined a group of five ascetics who were living in complete detachment from the world. These men believed that the ultimate freedom of the mind could only be achieved by breaking the strength of the physical body and the various attachments of the senses. This idea appealed to the wandering prince and with typical directness and enthusiasm he launched himself into the new way of life. Following the example of his five new friends, he began to practice very severe austerities. In his zeal he quickly surpassed them, pushing himself to the very limits of his physical strength and endurance. He practiced with grim determination, eating and sleeping only when overcome by hunger or exhaustion. His once strong body became weak and frail, his mind tortured with dreams and illusions. In brief moments of lucidity he saw that his practice was not having the desired effect. It seemed that the more he punished and mortified his body, the more intense his mental confusion and suffering became. Still he persevered. He could see no other path. But his doubts about the efficacy of his ascetic life would not go away. Eventually he saw that asceticism was not a path to the Truth, but a path to death, and he knew that death was not the freedom he had been seeking.

That realization was a kind of turning point in Gautama Buddha's life. Until that time he had pursued the Truth as a kind of dream. That dream had led him to try all kinds of extreme practices; to endure great pain, discomfort, and hardship. But now he realized that such extreme practices could never lead him to peace, happiness, or a balanced view of life.

So, without regret or explanation, he left the place of ascetic practice and began to wander along the course of a small river. Soon he met a girl who was carrying a pot of milk. When the girl saw the gaunt figure of the prince she knew that he needed food. She offered him her milk, and he accepted it and drank it gratefully. Almost immediately he felt the strength returning to his tortured body. He felt relaxed and comfortable for the first time in years. Then he understood, in a direct and simple way, the great importance of food and drink in the lives of human beings. He saw for the first time that a healthy body and a peaceful mind are one and the same. So he resolved to begin a new life, a simple and moderate life of simple and moderate activities. He found a nice tree near the bank of the river, and under its protective branches he prepared a comfortable seat. When he sat on the seat he settled naturally into the cross-legged posture which had become so familiar to him during his years of ascetic training. Now, however, he sat without any particular aim or intention. He just sat—quietly and peacefully.

In the quietness of that peaceful state, Gautama Buddha could see what was really there. He saw trees and rocks and leaves. He heard birds singing. He felt the beating of his heart and the coolness of sweat upon his brow. He saw and felt everything just as it was. And it was splendid.

Early one morning as he sat on his seat beneath the tree, he saw a lone star shining brightly in the east sky. At that moment he found that the whole universe was splendid and alive. Each star, each tree, each blade of grass participated equally in the perfection which was the world. And Buddha knew that this perfection was the Truth he had been seeking for so many years. He knew then, without any doubt or uncertainty, that the Truth was present in every thing, in every place, at every moment. And he knew that the way to find that Truth—the way to know and experience that Truth—was to participate directly in the unfolding reality of life. It was to lose oneself in action, in doing. It was, for example, to sit with all one's heart and mind. Sitting, just sitting in the ancient posture of the Masters' was, for Gautama Buddha, the gate to the splendid world, the gate to the real world. It was the Truth itself.

Buddha knew that this practice, this Truth, was something which should belong to the whole world, to all humanity. He wanted to share his discovery with the world, and yet he hesitated. He hesitated because the Truth was so simple, so very simple that is it was almost impossible to talk about, almost impossible to explain. But after some consideration he decided that he must try. He first thought of returning to his Masters, but he learned that both of them had died, so he decided to visit his former friends who were still engaged in their ascetic practices. When they saw him coming toward their camp, they were surprised and angry. They regarded him as a traitor and a coward, a man who had given up his ascetic vows because of personal weakness. So they quickly resolved to ignore the traitor who was returning to his former home. "We must be silent," they said. "We must not speak if he dares come here." But when the Buddha came and stood quietly before them, they saw a different person from the frail prince who had wandered away from their camp. The man standing before them was a new man, a splendid man. His body was strong, his face radiant, yet composed. He seemed to embody the qualities of peace, contentment, and dignity. Forgetting their promise, the five friends opened their circle making a place for the Buddha to sit.

Then Gautama Buddha began to speak. He spoke with the honesty and conviction of a man who has experienced the fullness of life; a man who has gone through all the phases of human experience and understanding; and who, having lived through those phases, has found a special vantage point from which to view his own life, the lives of others, and the Truth itself.

Thus, the Buddha's first lecture followed the outline of these phases of understanding, these separate aspects or faces of the Truth. It is said that his lecture was an explication of four fundamental ideas or philosophies: Four Noble Truths. In the earliest scriptures these four truths are outlined very simply and somewhat enigmatically as the Truth of Suffering, the Truth of Accumulation or Aggregation, the Truth of Negation, and the Truth of the Way, the Path, or simply the Truth itself.

Later scriptures contain many interpretations of these four truths, but I believe that most of those interpretations are wrong or, at best, misleading. So here I would like to suggest a new interpretation of the Four Noble Truths. It is an interpretation based primarily on my own experience of life and on my study of the philosophical works of Master Dogen. It is also based on my belief that, in his first lecture to his former friends, Gautama Buddha would have gone to great pains to explain a coherent theory: a theory which could encompass the complexities of life—the real and difficult problems of living—while suggesting a logical way of looking at and dealing with those complexities, both in theory and in practical life. Of course we have no way of knowing exactly how Gautama Buddha chose to explain his understanding of life to his five friends that day, but I am convinced that the interpretation which follows contains the essence of his thought—the essence of Buddhism itself.

At the beginning we must recognize the fundamental character of human beings. We are thinking beings, beings which think. Thinking is a kind of activity which produces images devoid of substance. At times those images appear to be real, but in fact they are not. They are only dreams, only reflections of the real world. At the first phase of our lives we are usually fascinated by these dream-like images. We want to know their source. In looking for that source we discover the mind, the self, or some symbolic representation of the mind or spirit: a god or a demon. At this phase we usually have a childlike innocence, an ability to believe in the ideas and images of the mind without doubt or question. We believe that all things are possible for we can find no limits to our thought. We have many hopes and many dreams. We want to realize them all.

TO MEET THE REAL DRAGON

Gautama Buddha esteemed the value of the hopes and dreams of human beings. He knew that without dreams they can have no ambition, no impulse to work or to learn. But at some stage the real nature of dreams has to be learned. Sooner or later we must recognize that dreams are not the real world. This learning process is usually quite painful. It is very painful to realize that we cannot get what we want; that, no matter what we do, our dreams will never be realized. Each and every human being must make this discovery for himself. Each and every human being must suffer from the conflict between dreams and reality. Suffering is, in fact, the most notable characteristic of human life at the first phase of understanding. This is why Gautama Buddha called his first truth, the Truth of Suffering.

The discovery of a world which is different from dreams, ideas, and mental images is the starting point of the second phase of human understanding. At this phase people begin to look at things in a more objective manner. The self-conscious awareness of the mind or the subject begins to subside, and in its place the concrete world of facts, things, and matter appears. At this phase of understanding, Gautama Buddha urged his friends to look at the world very precisely; to consider how the world is constructed; to see what it is made of and how it actually works.

Such precise observations of the world lead naturally to an awareness of the divisible nature of things—to the notion that all things are composed of parts; that these parts are in turn composed of smaller parts; that these small parts can be further broken down to their constituent elements; and so on and on until one finds (in theory) the infinitely small and undifferentiated bits of matter out of which the entire universe is is constructed.

And what determines the final shape which these bits of matter assume? How does the universe, as we know it, come to exist? It is by the action of a stern and unbending rule: the rule of cause and effect. All things which appear in this world do so as a result of a chain of past events. These chains of cause and effect evolve and build on each other, forming an inter-connected web of causal relations. The entire universe can thus be seen as an accumulation, an aggregate product of these interconnected chains of cause and effect.

Following such a line of thought leads to a very deterministic view of life, but one which is very hard to dispute. Such a view had many ardent proponents at the time of Gautama Buddha's discovery of the Truth, and when he tried to explain that Truth to his friends, he asked them to consider these materialistic theories very carefully. He asked them to observe the action of cause and effect in their own lives. He urged them to see and understand the "Truth of Aggregation": the philosophy which explains and exposes the material face of the universe.

Having explained this objective face of reality, Gautama Buddha pointed out an interesting fact. He asked his friends to notice that a philosophy based on the sensory perception of the uni-verse has no place for the mind or spirit of man. So if we want to believe in the world of mind or spirit, we must reject all theories based on objective perception and research. If, on the other hand, we want to believe in those objectively based theories and philosophies, we must deny as illusions the insub-stantial images and dreams of the mind.

This conflict or contradiction between the two views of reality was really an intolerable situation—a situation which had to be overcome if people were to live at peace with themselves and in harmony with others. Somehow a new philosophy or viewpoint had to be forged which could account for and accomodate these two conflicting views of the world.

So Gautama Buddha proposed a new way of thinking about the world. It was a theory or philosophy which resolved the appar-ent conflict between the mental world and the physical world by recognizing the time and place the two worlds meet. That time is now. That place is here. Here and now we are living. Here and now we are doing something; we are acting. When we act, the self and the external world are combined into oneness. In action, the one real world appears. Thus, Gautama Buddha's new theory might be called the theory of action. The theory of action in the here and now was the center of Gautama Buddha's new understanding of life. It was, in effect, his resolution of the conflict between idealism and materialism.

This new theory was thus a partial rejection of the first two phases of our understanding of life. It was a rejection of the idea that we must rely on only one view of the world. This is why the third noble truth was called the "Truth of Negation." It was a negation of the extremes in favor of a synthesis of the two—a synthesis which revealed a third point of view: the philosophy of action.

We can see then that Gautama Buddha's explanation of the Truth was based on the interrelations between three separate views of reality: the first based on dreams, the second on sensory perception, and the third on action in the here and now. To begin we must have our dreams. Without our dreams we can never discover the existence of a world which is different from the world of dreams and ideas, that is, the world as perceived by the senses. When we discover the world of the senses, our lives lose their freshness and vitality. We are depressed and discouraged by the rigidity of the rule of cause and effect. We have no freedom. We lose interest in life itself. So we need to find a new basis for our lives and we can find that basis in action. But the real meaning of the philosophy of action can only be found by observing the dynamic interplay of ideas and perceptions which arise from the contradictory viewpoints of idealism and materialism.

The relations between the three views of reality are thus very complex and somewhat ironic, but without even one we cannot find the meaning of our lives. Without dreams we cannot begin our journey. Without the senses we cannot learn about the objective realities of life. And without the philosophy of action, we can never resolve the conflict between these two contradictory aspects of life and our understanding of life.

So we need all three viewpoints to complete our understanding of life. But an understanding of life is not life itself. Life is not theories, philosophies, or fancy logic. Life is something else entirely. It is something we can neither name nor describe with certainty. It is something ineffable. Gautama Buddha recognized this fact very clearly. He saw that we are not living in theories or philosophies, but in the ineffable reality itself. He knew that if we want to know this reality, we must experience it—we must realize it directly. Without the direct realization of reality, all theories and philosophies are useless weeds floating on the water of life.

So Gautama Buddha urged his friends to transcend reliance on intellectual theories about the world and to enter the real world directly. To do that, he recommended the ancient posture of the masters': the simple posture or practice known as *dhyana* in India, *ch'an* in China, and zazen here in Japan. He explained that the simple act of sitting in the posture of the patriarchs was itself the complete realization of the Truth. It was the realization *and practice* of the Truth. It was the true gate to the real world.

This fourth and final truth was the culmination of Gautama Buddha's first lecture. It was the culmination of his unique conception of life and the universe. It is said that when his five friends heard this lecture, they realized that they were listening to the Truth itself. They were moved to abandon their ascetic way of life and become disciples of their former companion. And so, Gautama Buddha's career as a master or teacher of the Truth had begun. After teaching his friends, he began to wander about India expressing through his words and actions the Truth which is to be found in the real world. Since he was living in that world at every moment, he was alive to the possibilities inherent in every situation. His teachings were thus direct and spontaneous reactions to the people and situations he encountered in his travels. Many people were touched by that directness. They found in the Buddha a man of compassion and sincerity who gave his teachings freely, without concern for himself. To many, he seemed a perfect man, and in a sense he was. The Buddha was perfect, not in the sense of an ideal, but in the sense that he was simply what he was—completely and utterly human, perfectly human. Such perfection is not an ideal because it exists in each of us, right here, right now. Gautama Buddha taught us how to find that perfection. He taught us how to find ourselves and how to become the masters of ourselves through the practice of zazen. In other words, he taught us how to become the same person as himself: a Buddha in the real world.

A Buddha is, then, not a superman or a god. He must live his life according to the laws of the universe. Gautama Buddha lived, taught, and experienced life very simply and naturally. When he was about eighty years old, he contracted dysentery and died—a quiet death in the presence of a few of his disciples.

QUESTIONS & ANSWERS

You mentioned that realizing the futility of ascetic practices was a turning point in Gautama Buddha's life. Was it in fact his attainment of enlightenment?

No, I don't think so. Perhaps we can say it was a kind of enlightenment. Whenever we gain some clear insight into our real situation in life, it is a kind of enlightenment. Such insights are very important, but they are not the fundamental enlightenment of Buddhism. Enlightenment, in the Buddhist tradition, is not an intellectual discovery, but a state of being or a state of body and mind. It is a state of momentary oneness with the world—a state in which dualistic interpretations fall away and the real qualities of all things are exposed. It is, in other words, the state in zazen.

GAUTAMA BUDDHA

So, Gautama Buddha's actual attainment of the Truth was contained in the simple and direct act of sitting. When he sat
down under the Bodhi tree with no intention other than to sit,
that was, in itself, his attainment of the Truth. Later, when
he came to consciously realize or appreciate that fact, he
attained the Truth in another sense. That was his conscious
recognition of the splendid world, here and now. So we can
think that Gautama Buddha's attainment of the Truth came in two
stages. The first was when he entered the real world directly
through the practice of zazen. The second was when he recognized the beauty of sitting quietly in this world.

*Buddha found the Truth after giving up his ascetic practices.
Were those practices actually a hindrance to him, or were they
a necessary part of his journey? Is it necessary for us to go
through some painful period in order to see the Truth?*

The final conclusion of Buddhism is that sitting in quietness
is the Truth itself. This simple fact was the ultimate discovery of Gautama Buddha, and it has been confirmed by all true
masters from his time to the present day. Before Buddha there
was no such theory; no one had clearly seen the fundamental
nature of reality and then passed the discovery on to others.
So, to understand Gautama Buddha's life story, we must realize
that he was a kind of pioneer. He was searching for the Truth
without a guide. He had no way of knowing whether a particular
path or philosophy would lead to the Truth or not. Asceticism
was popular among religious seekers of his day. Buddha could
not discover the effectiveness of such practices by thinking
about them. He had to actually try them himself. When we think
of Guatama Buddha in this way, that is, as a pioneer or perhaps
as a scientist, we can appreciate the fact that all of his
experiences in life were important and useful to him.

Fundamentally speaking, we are all in the same situation. At
the beginning of our search for the Truth, we cannot know what
the Truth is. So we have to take some risks. We have to try
something. In our lives we encounter many complicated and con-

fusing problems. If we are to learn, we must be willing to
wrestle with those problems, to work with them. When we do, our
experiences in life become stepping stones on the way to the
Truth, and, as such, they are very important and useful to us.
So we shouldn't be too hesitant in our search. If we worry that
we will make mistakes or follow the wrong path, we will waste
our lives away in thinking and dreaming. We must open ourselves
to life and have faith that life itself will show us the correct path. To follow such a path of trail and error is to live
the Buddhist life.

*Wasn't there something selfish about Gautama Buddha's decision
to become a monk? He left his home and his responsibilities
there in order to find something for himself, didn't he? Wasn't
he looking for some kind of personal salvation?*

In the Buddhist scriptures, it is said that Gautama Buddha left
his home and sought the Truth in order to save all sentient
beings. He is portrayed as the epitome of selflessness, and his
years of asceticism are cited as evidence of his lack of personal ambition. But I'm afraid such a portrayal is a little
one-sided. I cannot believe that Gautama Buddha was completely
devoid of selfish motives. His seach for the Truth was as
likely prompted by his own confusion and pain as by his wish to
help other people. So, I think it is a mistake to criticize
Buddha for selfishness, but at the same time, we should not be
misled by notions of idealistic saintliness. In fact, Buddha
was both selfish and altruistic, or perhaps we should say
that he was neither selfish nor altruistic. He was simply
Gautama Buddha: a real man in the real world seeking the meaning of his life.

*I am personally interested in this problem of selfishness. Some
of my friends have said that Buddhism itself is selfish because
it encourages us to work on ourselves. They think that zazen
leads to an inward-looking emphasis on the self. They say that
if I were really concerned about other people, I would get out
and do something for them. Sometimes I feel confident that*

studying Buddhism is the right thing for me to do, but at other times their criticism strikes home. Sometimes I really do feel selfish.

You are teaching English here in Japan, aren't you?

Yes, I am.

Are you well-paid?

Fairly well, I guess.

I see...and when you are teaching your students do you think about the money you are making?

Perhaps sometimes, but usually I'm too busy teaching.

Then, do you do your best to teach your students?

Yes, I try...

Well then, I think there is no particular problem. You are a teacher. You work to make money for your life, but at the same time, you sincerely want to teach your students; you are work-ing for them. I think life is always like this. It always has a selfish side and an altruistic side. In fact, I think it is impossible to be purely selfish or purely altruistic in our conduct. So if we try to determine whether we are being selfish or not, we will always have a problem. If we look at our lives from one side, we appear to be altruistic; but if we look at our lives from another side, we seem to be selfish. We have a tendency to wobble back and forth, left and right. We can't find our balance.

Most religions urge us to be altruistic. They say that to be altruistic is good—to be selfish is bad. But this is not the Buddhist understanding. Buddhism suggests that we need not worry whether we are selfish or not. To analyze our actions intellectually only pulls us from side to side and leads us from the Middle Way, from the real situation. When we are living sincerely, moment by moment, our lives unfold naturally and the question of selfishness does not arise. So according to Buddhism, our task is not to analyze, but to live—to really live. We must get into the river of life or, in Master Dogen's words, we must stay in the water. To stay in the water is to live sincerely in the world as it is without being concerned that it is the right world or the wrong world, the good world or the bad. When we transcend the difference between selfishness and altruism, we find the real world as it is. We enter reality itself.

I would like to know more about your "new" interpretation of the Four Noble Truths. In all the books I've read about Buddhism, the Four Noble Truths have been explained in relation to suffering, the cause of suffering, and the way to eventual liberation from suffering; so I find it rather difficult to relate such ideas to your description of Gautama Buddha's first lecture to his friends.

Yes, I can understand your confusion. The interpretation of the Four Noble Truths which you have just described is very famous. In most books about Buddhism, the four truths are outlined in a very simple schema of cause and effect. According to that schema the first truth is the truth of suffering. Our lives are filled with pain, anguish, and disappointment. Life is suffering. The second truth is that suffering has a cause and that cause is desire. So the third truth states that the way to resolve the problem of suffering is to eliminate desire. And the final truth is the noble path or way which, if followed sincerely, will lead to the negation of desire, the ending of suffering, and the revelation of the Truth itself.

When I first encountered this theory, I felt that something was wrong. Of course there was suffering in the world, but was life only suffering? Was there no happiness or satisfaction, no simple joy in the world? And how could life exist without desire? To me, life and desire were indivisible; they were simply two sides of the same coin. If Gautama Buddha really urged us to get rid of desire, it seemed that he was urging us to do the impossible. So, from the very first, I had strong doubts about the traditional interpretation of the Four Noble Truths. I could not believe that it was really the ultimate theory of the founder of the Buddhist religion.

When I began to study the *Shōbōgenzō*, I searched for some explanation of the Four Noble Truths, but I could find no theory which resembled that rather simple philosophy. Instead I found that Master Dogen looked at all problems in Buddhism from a variety of philosophical viewpoints. Eventually I discovered that there was a kind of pattern or logic in his use of those viewpoints. That logic consisted of four stages. At the first stage, he always looked at a problem or theory from the viewpoint of the subject or self; in other words, from an idealistic standpoint. Then he would study the same problem objectively, or from a materialistic standpoint. At the third stage, he would examine the problem from a standpoint which transcended the separation of subject and object. This was the viewpoint which I call the Buddhist philosophy of action. Finally, Master Dogen would point beyond theoretical considerations to something very real, very substantial, yet ultimately unexplainable: reality itself.

In chapter after chapter of the *Shōbōgenzō* I found the same logic, the same pattern of thinking—and one day it occurred to me that this logic must be the real foundation of all Buddhist theory. If this were so, I felt that there must be some direct relationship between the four philosphical viewpoints in the *Shōbōgenzō* and the original theories of Gautama Buddha. So I studied the Four Noble Truths to see if such a relationship might exist. I found that in the earliest scriptures, the exact meaning of the Four Noble Truths was not clearly defined. There was a quality of vagueness which seemed strange to me in view of the rather dogmatic tone of later scriptures. It was as if the scribes who first attempted to record the teachings of

Gautama Buddha were themselves unsure what his original intent had been. The vagueness of these early scriptures was, in fact, encouraging to me, for it led me to believe that the Four Noble Truths could be interpreted more broadly than the later Sutras and commentaries suggested. I also found that many aspects of Gautama Buddha's life and teachings became clear and under- standable if the Four Noble Truths were interpreted on the basis of Master Dogen's four viewpoints. Those discoveries, coupled with Master Dogen's own insistence that his teachings were, in every respect, identical to those of Gautama Buddha, led me to conclude that the traditional interpretation of the Four Noble Truths was an unfortunate misunderstanding, a mis- understanding which could only be corrected by substituting a rather radical reinterpretation of the same four truths.

This conclusion was startling, even to me, and I was somewhat frightened by its implications. I had no particular desire to be a reformer or to challenge the traditional beliefs of a religion I admired and esteemed. But at the same time I felt that the Truth must have priority over any other consideration. So for a time I simply adopted my new interpretation of the Four Noble Truths as a kind of working hypothesis and I con- tinued my study of Buddhism on that basis for many years. Finally the hypothesis became my firm belief. I believe that Gautama Buddha's original intent was not to explain the problem of suffering alone, but to show the real nature of life as it is viewed from four separate and distinct standpoints. We now have the ability to identify and describe those distinct views of the world very clearly and precisely. Thus, I usually ex- plain the Four Noble Truths in terms of four philosophies. The four philosophies are idealism, materialism, the philosophy of action, and the philosophy of a Truth beyond philosohy: the ineffable reality itself.

If you have read many books about Buddhism, it may, at this point, be difficult for you to accept my interpretation of the Four Noble Truths, but I hope you will try to keep an open mind. Before we are finished, I hope to show that many of the original theories of Buddhism do in fact reflect this understanding. I also hope to show that my interpretation has more than theoretical value. I believe that if Buddhism is to have real value in our lives, it must provide a means of working with our real problems. Those problems are not so simple. Our lives are complicated and confused. If we want to live well, we need a means of understanding the complexities of our lives. I think that Gautama Buddha tried to give us such a means when he taught the Four Noble Truths to his friends and disciples. And I believe that his purpose is fulfilled when we understand the Four Noble Truths following my theory of four philosophies.

Your use of modern philosophical terms to explain Buddhism is interesting, but aren't you in danger of distorting the original meaning? It seems to me that if we use concepts to explain Buddhism which did not exist when Buddha lived, then our understanding will be different from his.

It is true that at the time Gautama Buddha lived there were no philosophical concepts of idealism, materialism, the theory of action, and so on. But we should remember that such concepts are only methods of explaining what we experience in our lives. Faced with the diversity of such experiences, it sometimes seems incredible that we can communicate at all. But in fact we can and do, and this suggests that underlying all human experience there is a common foundation, a common ground. This is the Buddhist belief. We believe, as Buddhists, that our lives are not so very different from Gautama Buddha's life. We believe that our experience of life is fundamentally the same as his even though we have many new ways of explaining that experience.

Gautama Buddha found that life had four dimensions. He had no exact concepts to explain the differences between those dimensions, so he tried to explain his understanding through a simple theory of four truths. Unfortunately, the independent dignity of the four truths was not understood by many of the followers of the Buddha. They interpreted the four truths to be a single theory which described a chain of cause and effect. This fundamental misunderstanding has plagued Buddhism through the centuries.

Fortunately, our understanding of philosophy has progressed greatly from the time Gautama Buddha lived. We have many new tools to use in explaining our experience of life. We need not hesitate to use those tools simply because they did not exist 2,500 years ago. We must try to understand our lives according to the progress of our thought today. We must try to understand Buddhism with our own method of thinking. Buddhism itself can never change. The experience and the fundamental recognition of that experience are forever the same, but the method of explaining that experience and that recognition must change and evolve to suit the conditions of the time. I believe that Buddhism can be understood more clearly today than ever before, *if* we use all the tools which are available to us. I believe that the Four Noble Truths are in fact the philosophical viewpoints of idealism, materialism, the philosophy of action, and the ineffable reality itself. And I believe the the true meaning of Buddhist theory can only come alive if we understand the Four Noble Truths in this way.

What do you mean when you say that life and desire are two sides of the same coin?

Buddhism begins with the belief that something exists. It is an ineffable something—an indivisible something which cannot be precisely defined with words. Nevertheless, it is our nature as human beings to consider all things intellectually: to divide the ineffable into parts and, having done so, to apply names and concepts to what we find. Through such a process we may discover the existence of desire, and we may conceive of it as something different from life. When we divide life and desire in our thought, desire tends to become something embarrassing, something dirty or profane. But when we experience desire as it is, it can have no such meaning. This is because, in the real world, life and desire cannot be divided. Where there is life, there is desire; and where there is no desire, there is no life. This is the fact in this world. Precisely speaking, life and desire are only concepts or ideas. In the real world life and desire are combined into one fact: they are just two faces of one thing. We can call that one thing reality, or life, or desire itself. Thus, in Buddhism, desire is not some embarrassing factor in our lives, but our life itself. It is something pure or sacred. It is just the Truth itself.

THE TRANSMISSION OF THE TRUTH

I hope that in our last discussion you were able to get a feeling for Gautama Buddha as a real man in history. I think it is
important to know the story of his life and to understand that
he was not a god or a superman, but an ordinary person like
ourselves: a man who experienced the pleasures and pains of
life on this earth. Having established such an understanding,
I think we should now go a step further; I think we should look
for a more direct and immediate connection between ourselves
and the man called Buddha. I feel such a connection myself very
strongly. It is a feeling which has arisen from my years of
study and practice, and I believe the feeling is based on something real. I believe that there is a real connection between
ourselves and Gautama Buddha. I would like to try to explain
that connection now.

One of the most important facts we learn by studying the life
of Gautama Buddha is that, after attaining the Truth, he was
not content to enjoy the fruits of his realization alone. He
felt compelled to share his experience and understanding with
the world. He wanted to bring people out of the world of suffering and confusion, and into the real world—his world—the
world of Buddha.

Many scriptures praise Gautama Buddha as the one who, out of

compassion for his follow man, chose to remain in the world
rather than stepping directly into *nirvana*: the realm of eternal bliss. This account of Buddha's compassion and selflessness
has some elements of truth, but I feel that it is a little too
idealistic. I believe that Gautama Buddha began his teaching
because he had already entered nirvana. In my understanding,
nirvana is not a mystical realm or mysterious planet, but the
real world itself. In the real world, the true relatedness of
all things was clearly visible to Gautama Buddha. He saw the
external world and the people in it, not as something separate
from himself, but as part of himself. Thus, to work for the
benefit of others was, at the same time, to work for the benefit of himself. Therefore, we can say that his ministry began,
not as the supremely altruistic act which is recorded in the
sutras, but as a supremely natural act. It was like taking food
or drinking water. It was the natural activity of a man awake
in the real world.

I think the people he met in his travels could recognize that
quality. They sensed that his actions were undertaken without
regard to any personal ambition, but according to some wider
necessity. In other words, they could sense the purity of the
man and his intentions. Wherever he went, people gathered to
see and hear the Buddha: the awakened one. They were touched by
his words and his presence. They came to him spontaneously and
asked to be accepted as his disciples. And Buddha accepted them
in the same spirit. He welcomed all people equally, for all
people were the same in his eyes.

The search for spiritual truth was highly esteemed in Indian
society at that time. Gautama Buddha's renunciation of his
family and social ties was not a rare or isolated case, but, in
fact, a rather common practice among those who, for one reason
or another, had become dissatisfied with their lives in society. The homeless life, free of attachment to material com-
forts, was an ideal which had inspired many sincere seekers.
Many of Gautama Buddha's disciples were leading such a life
when they met him, and it was natural for them to continue to

live in that style as they followed him in his wanderings. Many other people were inspired to follow the example of Gautama Buddha and his followers; in a short time a kind of monastic order had come into being. Of course, not all of the Buddha's followers were inclined to give up their homes, families, and jobs. Many preferred to study and practice within the context of their everyday lives in society. These lay followers, along with the monks and nuns of the monastic order, formed the Sangha: the Buddhist community.

Every community must have some rules if its members are to live together harmoniously. Buddha's disciples often came to him with questions about personal or social problems. He always welcomed such questions, for he felt that the problem of how to live was the central issue in life. His advice was practical and down to earth: we should do this; we should not do that. He suggested such rules as guidelines for living. Those rules or precepts were eventually formalized, and persons wishing to enter the Sangha "received" the precepts as the mark of beginning a new life. Such rules and ceremonies contributed to the Sangha's sense of community and to the development of Buddhism as a religious institution.

There are certain dangers which seem to be inherent in the establishment of religious groups or institutions. One of those is that the members of the community are inclined to lose sight of the real nature of their institution. They tend to confuse the external form of the religion with the religion itself. In their eyes the rules, ceremonies, and other visible aspects of the religion take on paramount importance. Gautama Buddha, himself, never suffered from such delusions. He recognized the real value of the community which had evolved naturally around him. It provided an environment in which people could come into contact with the teachings and, from there, find their way to the Truth itself. Teaching the Truth, showing people how to find the Truth in their own lives, through their own efforts, was the aim of Gautama Buddha's life. The Sangha provided a means of accomplishing that aim. It was like a vehicle or carriage which carried the Truth into the world. It was a good vehicle, a practical vehicle. As it grew, more and more people came into contact with the teachings and Buddhism prospered.

The Sangha included people of all types from all walks of life. As they entered the Buddhist community, they brought with them the innate qualities of their personalities, along with the accumulated experience, knowledge, and problems of their lives. Some of them were scholars who studied the teachings earnestly but could not understand the importance of physical practice. Others were very practical people, who found in zazen a means of harmonizing their everyday lives, but who had little interest in the theoretical aspects of the teachings. There were also a few very sincere disciples who devoted themselves wholeheartedly to both areas of Buddhist life. As they followed the Buddha, day after day, intellectual study and physical practice became the natural activities of their lives. It was their daily work. Very slowly and subtly, their minds and bodies changed until, finally, the distinction between themselves as disciples and Gautama Buddha as master seemed to dissolve. There was no longer anything separating them. They had, in a sense, become the same person.

When Buddha realized that such a situation had evolved, he held a ceremony to formally certify their realization. The ceremony was a recognition of the understanding which had been attained, and a formal acknowledgement that the Dharma had been transmitted to a new Buddha. Among those who received the transmission of the Truth, Gautama Buddha saw that the one called Maha-Kasyapa was his most excellent disciple, and so, before he died, he named Maha-Kasyapa as his Dharma-heir: his successor as head of the Buddhist order. Maha-Kasyapa in turn transmitted the Truth and the order to Ananda. Ananda was succeeded by Sanavasa who transmitted the Dharma to Upagupta. In this way, a direct line of succession was established which united the transmission of the Truth and the Transmission of the order.

This principle worked well for a time, but there were, in

reality, many lines of transmission. The teachings of Buddhism
radiated out from their source in many directions. The disciples of Gautama Buddha taught their own disciples according
to their own understanding and experience of the Truth. Many
schools or sects developed around those masters, and each school
took on slightly different characteristics based on the master's individual manner of presenting the teachings. This eventually led to considerable diversity within the Buddhist institution and some confusion as to the essential foundations of
the religion itself. Many issues relating to the theory and
practice of Buddhism emerged and were vigorously debated by the
followers of the various schools.

Amid the debates and confusion, there were always a few excellent masters who tapped the original spring of Buddhism. In
their practice they were able to find the true link between
themselves and Gautama Buddha. When they experienced that sense
of personal connection with original Buddhism, they were no
longer confused by the intellectual or political issues of
their time. In zazen, they had found the real basis of Buddhism, and that discovery gave them the supreme confidence of
knowing the Truth. That confidence was reflected in their
teachings which cut through theoretical arguments and pointed
the way directly to the real world. Wherever such masters
appeared, true Buddhism also appeared. In them the true transmission was confirmed and the true succession from Gautama
Buddha was continued.

One such master was known as Bodhidharma. After attaining the
Truth in India, he was inspired to carry the teachings of
Gautama Buddha to China. He was not the first Buddhist to go to
China, but those who preceeded him had transmitted only the
external form of the religion. When Bodhidharma arrived in
China, he found people discussing Buddhst theory and performing
Buddhist rituals, but he could find no one who practiced in the
posture of Gautama Buddha. Bodhidharma had little time for
scholarly discussion. Buddhism was for him something active,
something to be found in a life of practice. So he taught that

the original practice of Gautama Buddha was the center of Buddhism itself. He taught with words and he taught through his sincere example. Legends claim that he sat facing a wall for nine years. The story is clearly an exaggeration, but it reveals Bodhidharma's reverence for practice as the essential foundation of Buddhist life.

It is said that the Chinese people found the actions of the Master from India rather queer. He was ridiculed by teachers of other religions; but a man who lives a life of practice has an inner strength, or power, which will always overcome deluded people who have never experienced the Truth. Eventually, Bodhidharma triumphed over the skeptics and scholars, and succeeded in transmitting true Buddhism to China.

From Bodhidharma the transmission passed on to the great patriarchs of Chinese Buddhism. Around them Buddhism grew and prospered. Many disciples studied, practiced, and attained the Truth. Many monasteries were built, and they became important centers of learning. Chinese civilization as a whole was thus influenced by the presence of Buddhism, and the Buddhist institution itself came to have uniquely Chinese characteristics. Unfortunately, as had been the case in India, the Buddhist institution often strayed from the essential teachings of its founders.

When Master Dogen went to China, he was at first very disappointed. The great monasteries seemed to be in a state of decline. The masters he met and their teachings seemed little better than those of his native Japan. He could find nothing new, nothing which promised to bring him nearer the Truth. But when he met Master Nyojō, he felt that at last he had met a master firmly in touch with the original mind and body of Gautama Buddha. Later he understood the basis of his intuitive feeling. He understood that in the real world there is only one Buddhism, and that the one true Buddhism manifests itself in the master who is living in that world. Such a master always knows the essence of Buddhism. He is always prepared to transmit that essence to a sincere and willing disciple. To meet such a master is a wonderful event. Master Dogen loved his Master, and he esteemed the great lineage of Indian and Chinese patriarchs who had transmitted the Truth to him.

After receiving the transmission from Master Nyojō, Master Dogen returned to Japan, confident that he had found, received, and realized the one true Buddhism of Gautama Buddha. He had no doubts or misgivings. He knew that his task was to continue the transmission which had begun nearly 2,000 years before.

He set about his task very directly and without compromise. He taught what he knew to be the essence of Buddhism, and he criticized any theory or practice which did not contain that essential Truth. Buddhism was not the worship of gods or the appeasement of demons. It was not the chanting of Buddha's name, the reading of sutras, or the burning of incense. It was not the extinction of desire or the complete elimination of the consciousness of the self. Such beliefs and practices were not true Buddhism. True Buddhism, according to Master Dogen, was to be found in the real world, and teachings, to be true, had to point the way to that world directly.

The real world is the world of Gautama Buddha. We can enter that world ourselves. We can experience Gautama Buddha's world at any moment. When we take the posture of Gautama Buddha, we become Buddhas at once. That is our direct connection with Gautama Buddha. It is our connection with the Truth. It is Buddhism itself.

This was the essence of Master Dogen's teachings. He taught the same message in many ways and from many points of view throughout his life. In those years his confidence never wavered. The first time I read the *Shōbōgenzō*, I could feel that confidence even though I could understand nothing of the real meaning of his words. When, at last, I understood his words, I also found the source of his confidence. Master Dogen's confidence is now my confidence. I believe that Master Dogen's Buddhism is true

Buddhism, original Buddhism. I would like to continue his work to the best of my ability. I believe it is my simple duty to do so.

QUESTIONS AND ANSWERS

At times you speak of transmission as if it were a gradual process. At other times it seems to be a single event or a ceremony of some kind. Which is it really?

Actually, it is both. When a person becomes a Buddhist, he becomes the disciple of a master. During the course of their association, the disciple studies Buddhism and he studies the problems of his life as they arise. Gradually, through his study and practice, his body and mind change and the way he perceives the world also changes. He begins to discover what is real and what is illusion. His actions become more direct, more confident. Many former problems seem to dissolve, and new problems which arise have a simple concrete quality; they can be seen as simple challenges or inspirations for action. This is a quality of life in the real world which is, of course, the world of the master. And so the disciple has very slowly and subtly joined his master in the real world. To live in the real world is to live in the same mental and physical world as the master. In that world they can meet, talk, and act at the same level. In reality the master and disciple are not different. They have become the same. The disciple has become Buddha.

At that point the real transmission has already occurred, but the fact must be acknowledged. The situation must be confirmed, formally, correctly, according to tradition. The ceremony is held at night. In the ceremony, the master is Buddha. As Buddha, he has the authority to recognize Buddha in the person of the disciple. He confirms that the disciple is, in fact, Buddha; that he has already become Buddha. From that time on, the disciple is a master: a holder of the Truth. He has taken his place in the direct line of succession from Gautama Buddha.

THE TRANSMISSION OF THE TRUTH

If the real transmission of the Truth evolves naturally, as you have described, why is it necessary to have a formal ceremony at all?

The value of a formal ceremony is rather difficult to understand, especially from an idealistic point of view. When we talk about the transmission of the Truth, it seems very spiritual or mystical. We feel that such spiritual events are sacred and have no relation to the mundane facts of everyday life. This attitude leads us to devalue an important aspect of our real life. Buddhism has its spiritual side, of course, and the transmission of the Truth does involve something ineffable, something we can neither name nor describe; but at the same time, Buddhism always recognizes the value of practical facts in the real world.

The actual transmission has a quality of vagueness, rather like the transition from youth to adulthood. The ceremonial transmission confirms the transition. It sharpens the picture. It makes the situation clear and workable. So the formal ceremony has practical value, real value. Buddhism always affirms the value of the formal, traditional, practical facts of life.

Before I started coming to your lectures, I read some books about Buddhism and Buddhist history. I read about Hinayana and Mahayana Buddhism and the Tantric schools. I also learned that within those great divisions there are many schools, and the schools are composed of various sects and sub-sects, each with their own particular beliefs and practices. It seemed that the more I read, the more confusing Buddhism became. Finally, I decided that Buddhism was not one religion, but hundreds of small religions which share a few common ideas. Now I hear you say that Buddhism is only one, and it sounds a little strange. Can you explain?

Well, it's an excellent question. To find the answer we must clearly understand a distinction which I tried to point our earlier. As I said, people who are members of a religious institution have a tendency to believe that the institution is the religion itself. This is a misunderstanding. Most scholars and historians make this mistake too. It is a natural mistake for anyone who studies a religion intellectually. But the essence of a religion is not the institution which grows up around it, though of course it may reflect that essence. The essence of a religion is found in its fundamental beliefs and practices, and those beliefs and practices cannot be understood by spectators. Anyone who really wishes to understand a religion must find and experience the actual basis of its beliefs through the practice itself. This is something most scholars fail to do. Perhaps they fear that they will lose their objectivity, but unfortunately, unless they overcome those fears and actually enter into the religion personally, they will never know what they are talking about. Since they are lacking that personal experience, they can only study objective facts of the past. Those facts may be interesting, but without some personal criterion for judging their importance, they will never reveal their true relatedness and the religion will always remain an enigma.

When I began to study Buddhism, I also studied it intellectually, and found the great diversity of schools, teachings, and practices very confusing. But after I became a Buddhist and began to practice zazen, the essential nature of Buddhism began to be clear. Finally, I realized that true Buddhism is very simple and direct. It is not dependent on any particular teaching, or confined to any particular school or sect. It can be found wherever people sincerely seek the Truth through study and practice. We can find those simple elements right here and now in this room. Buddhism is very simple...there is only one Buddhism.

You seem to speak of religious institutions as a hinderance rather than as a necessary part of a religion, but some kind of institution is necessary, isn't it?

When Gautama Buddha attained the Truth, Buddhism was born. It

existed in him, and it has existed in all true masters since his
time. Whenever we follow their example and practice zazen sincerely, Buddhism is reborn at once. So, strictly speaking, an
institution is not absolutely necessary, but as a practical
matter, when people are brought together by a common interest,
and cooperate for the promotion of that interest, an institution is usually formed. It is a very natural process. So long
as an institution retains this original, organic, and practical
nature, it can serve the religion without hindering or altering
its fundamental practice. But institutions have a tendency to
become conservative and rigid.

We can see this tendency at the very beginning of Buddhist
history. When Gautama Buddha died, there was a feeling of great
loss in the Buddhist community. People wondered if Buddhism
could survive without the Master. They made efforts to preserve
his memory and teachings by telling and retelling stories of
his life. This was a very natural and sincere effort, but it
marked the beginning of a big change in Buddhism. That change
was from reliance on the direct teachings of a living master
to reliance on memory. Gautama Buddha's original teachings
were always suited to a particular place and time, a particular
situation. When they were reported from memory, they lost that
quality of freshness and appropriateness. They became fixed and
formal, a kind of dogma which was far removed from Buddha's
original intention.

The precepts also took on the same characteristics. They became
rigid rules rather than useful guidelines for living, and they
quickly multiplied until almost every aspect of community life
was regulated by some rule or law. In such a situation, Buddhist life itself became formal and lost much of its intrinsic
value. Fortunately, within the Buddhist institution, there were
masters who had received the true transmission of Buddhism.
They recognized the rigid quality of their institution, and
they sought to rekindle in it the original spirit of Gautama
Buddha. Eventually a split developed between those masters and
the elders who controlled the formal institution. This split

was the birth of Mahayana Buddhism. The emergence of Mahayana Buddhism restored the original character of the Buddhist teachings and brought new life to the Buddhist institution, but Mahayana Buddhism was not immune to the conservative tendency which had plagued the original institution. Actually, the problem is always present, and we must always be aware of our tendency to lose touch with true Buddhism. We must always remember that true Buddhism is something real—something active and alive. If our teachings and institutions lose contact with that source of life and vitality, they will become a hindrance rather than a helpful vehicle on the way to the Truth.

Do you feel that the Buddhist institutions in Japan reflect the original intent of Gautama Buddha?

There are many Buddhist institutions in Japan. They think their Buddhism is true Buddhism, but I don't think so. Perhaps I shouldn't express my opinion so bluntly, but I feel that very little true Buddhism remains in the Buddhist institutions of today. Of course, we can find many beautiful temples. Their libraries are filled with ancient sutras, and their halls are lined with beautiful art. Are these temples the homes of sincere Buddhist practice or museums full of relics from the past? If we look for the priest, we will usually find him busily performing funeral ceremonies or other traditional rites. Such activities have social value in the life of the community and practical value in that they provide a means of support for the priest and for the maintenance of his temple, but while these are important concerns, they are not central to the religion itself. Unfortunately, the priest often becomes so involved in these secular affairs that he has little time for study or practice. Without study and practice he quickly loses contact with the true source of his religion, and without that contact the religion itself becomes hollow and weak. Without a true master, where can Buddhism live?

So, I think the situation in Japan today is not so encouraging. Many people are involved in sincere efforts to preserve ancient temples and traditional ceremonies, but simply preserving monuments of the past cannot preserve Buddhism itself. This is very important.

Can true Buddhism re-emerge from the Buddhist institutions which exist now?

I would like to believe it is possible, but I cannot be optimistic in this regard. I believe that if we want to establish true Buddhism, we must begin a new movement based on the teachings of the *Shōbōgenzō* and the sincere practice of zazen. If we practice zazen every day, Buddhism will revive and flourish. We need not be concerned with reviving old institutions or creating new ones. Those problems will be solved naturally. What we must do is just practice zazen. Then we can find the rule of our life and the rule of the universe, and our actions will always be in accord with that rule. Then true Buddhism will live and grow naturally.

STARTING POINTS

I sometimes wonder about the Westerners who come to Japan to study Buddhism. I think many of them are looking for the heart of the mysterious Orient. Perhaps their day-to-day lives seem drab and uninteresting. They cannot find meaning in their social lives, and the religious institutions of their homelands seem to be part of that social situation. They are too familiar and ordinary, too boring and predictable. So they look for something new, something different. Zen Buddhism certainly seems different. It is full of strange stories, unfamiliar concepts, and unusual practices. It appears to to be mysterious and exotic. Such mystery is very appealing, but I am afraid it is an illusion. One of the purposes of these discussions is to dispel some of those illusions and misconceptions.

True Buddhism is not exotic or weird. True Buddhism is very simple, very practical, and very realistic. When we really understand Buddhism, we find that it is the other religions of the world which are strange and mysterious. They are mysterious because they are generally limited to one realm. That is the realm of thought, the realm of spirit or mind. In the realm of the mind, all things are possible, but in the real world there are real limits, practical limits like time and place. So the real world cannot be fantastic or strange. Reality is straight and simple. Reality is normal. Reality cannot be found at the extremities of thought and feeling. It can only be found at the point of balance between such extremes. Reality resides in the center or the middle, so in Buddhism we talk about the Middle Way.

The Middle Way is a very famous concept in Buddhism, and like most Buddhist ideas, it can be understood on many levels and from a variety of viewpoints. Many Buddhists explain the Middle Way as the way of living which lies between the extremes of an over-indulgent secular life and the overly strict and austere life of spiritual purity practiced by ascetics and priests. I think this understanding is true as far as it goes, and I think it reveals the origin of the concept in ancient India. At the time Gautama Buddha lived, there were two very different outlooks toward life. One school of thought was led by a group of naturalistic thinkers who became known as the six non-Buddhist priests. Their materialistic attitude naturally encouraged the pursuit of sensual gratification as the aim of life. At the other extreme were the Brahman priests and other idealistic religious seekers. They urged people to abandon sensual attachments and seek the liberation of the spirit through piety and prayer. Thus, in a philosophical sense, we can understand the Middle Way to be the attitude which lies between idealism and materialism. It is the attitude which rejects extreme viewpoints and extols the virtues of a moderate, balanced, and harmonious approach to life.

So the Middle Way is a very simple and straightforward idea. When we study the world and the people around us, we can easily see the suffering and disorder caused by the pursuit of excessive pleasure or unrealistic ideals. We often feel that our own lives are out of balance. We chase after unreachable goals or fleeting moments of enjoyment only to find disappointment and frustration. We can't seem to get what we want; often we can't even decide what it is we want. Sometimes we are excited and optimistic, at other times depressed and angry. In the ups and downs of such a life, we may begin to yearn for some discipline or order. Perhaps we should try to bring harmony into our lives. Perhaps we should follow the Middle Way.

It is a nice idea, but unfortunately, it is not so easy to accomplish. Following the Middle Way is not so simple as it sounds. This is an important point, one that we should not slide over lightly. Why is it difficult to follow the Middle Way? In one sense the problem is very simple. The problem is that the Middle Way is an intellectual concept, an ideal. It is not reality. It is not our life. Ideals are always unattainable simply because they are ideas and not reality.

We must wonder, then, why Gautama Buddha taught us to seek something which could not be attained in the real world. Why didn't he tell us to forget our ideals and just live in the ineffable reality? I'm afraid if he had done so, his followers would have stared at him with puzzled expressions on their faces. To seek something which is ineffable is contrary to our common sense. At the beginning of our study of Buddhism, we can have no clear sense of what "Dharma" or the ineffable reality might be. We need some mental image, some intellectual idea to grasp. This is our human nature. I think Gautama Buddha understood human nature very well. He understood that human beings always need something to work toward. They need a goal, an aim, or a target.

The Middle Way is such a target. To live a balanced, harmonious life, rejecting extreme views and actions is a goal we can easily grasp in our minds, if not in reality. The Middle Way is an ideal, but it is an ideal which reflects the real nature of the universe. Our efforts to live in the Middle Way will, in time, bring us into harmony with that universe. Then, at some point, we can transcend the ideal and live simply in the real world itself. Having a realistic aim is thus a necessary starting point for any human action or endeavor. In teaching the Middle Way, Gautama Buddha acknowledged that fact. To acknowledge the need for an aim is, in a broader sense, to acknowledge the importance of idealism in our lives. This is, I think, the real meaning of the Buddhist teaching of the Middle Way.

Master Dogen also acknowledged the importance of idealism, but in a different way. In the *Shōbōgenzō*, he often urges us to establish, nurture, and retain the will to the Truth. The will to the Truth is my translation of the Sanskrit word, *bodhicitta*. It is a very old concept in Buddhism, but in the works of Master Dogen it occupies a place of special importance. He insisted that the will to the Truth was an absolutely indispensable prerequisite to the study of Buddhism. We might have excellent knowledge of Buddhist theories and practices, but without the will to the Truth, such knowledge was absolutely useless. On the other hand, he asserted that once we have firmly established the will to the Truth, even though we make many errors and mistakes, those errors and mistakes will themselves become the cause of our attaining the Truth. When I first read such statements in the *Shōbōgenzō*, I understood that Master Dogen's belief in the will to the Truth was firm and uncompromising, but I could not understand why. I wondered why he had such reverence for the will to the Truth.

Now, in the light of my own experience, I can understand the reason for his uncompromising belief. I think we can find that reason in the story of his life. Master Dogen began to study Buddhism when he was very young. At that time he had no clear idea of what Buddhism really was. He had many foolish ideas and idealistic fantasies, but in fact, he could not understand Buddhism at all. He could not understand the sutras. He could not understand Buddhist theory. He could not understand the teachings of his masters. His thoughts about Buddhism were usually completely upside down and contrary to the intent of Gautama Buddha. He had no standard to separate truth from falsity, no realistic aim or target to work toward. In fact he had nothing—nothing but the will to the Truth.

And so the will to the Truth was itself the standard of his life. His mistaken ideas and fantasies themselves propelled him forward. As he encountered the realities of life, he experienced much pain and confusion, but that pain and confusion only increased his determination to find the Truth. Thus, in spite

of innumerable mistakes, misunderstandings, and personal difficulties, Master Dogen eventually reached the goal he had never
clearly seen in his mind. This was, for him, a remarkable fact.
When he thought about the experiences of his life, he could not
help feeling that his only true guide had been the will to the
Truth itself.

I think this is the reason Master Dogen esteemed the will to
the Truth so much. He believed that the will to the Truth is
our true ally, our true friend in life. To retain that ally is
thus the most important duty of human beings. We need not fear
pain, confusion, or great difficulties, but we should fear
losing the will to the Truth. Without the will to the Truth, we
can never arrive at the ultimate destiny of human life.

Of course we all have our particular problems, our peculiar
circumstances in life, but Master Dogen recognized that, in a
fundamental sense, those circumstances are all the same; that
we are all in the same boat together. We are like blind men
groping in the darkness of our confusion. There is no light, no
beacon to show us the way. We can only step forward in the
darkness. To step forward in the darkness is the will to the
Truth itself.

So the will to the Truth is very fundamental, very basic. It is
the restlessness which drives us on in our search for the meaning of life, the source of happiness, or a better way to live.
In this sense, then, all our efforts in life can be considered
to flow from the will to the Truth. When we begin to study
philosophy or religion, those efforts usually have a particular
quality or appearance. They are very pure, very spiritual, and
very idealistic. Master Dogen felt that such idealistic efforts
to understand our lives are the sincere and natural expression
of the will to the Truth. So Master Dogen did not reject idealism. Rather, he recognized it as one face of the human will to
know and understand. He felt that idealistic manifestations of
the will to the Truth are an important phase in the evolution
of human understanding.

I believe, then, that Master Dogen and Gautama Buddha had very similar attitudes toward idealism. They understood that, at first, human beings must be idealists. When people first meet Buddhism, they will always study it on the basis of idealistic thought. It is a necessary phase of human understanding, a natural stage in the process of learning about life and the problems of life. So Buddhism considers idealism to be the starting point of all thinking and understanding. It is not the final outcome or the ultimate Truth, but it is an important step on the way to that Truth. Without our dreams, ideas, and ideals, we could never begin our journey to the Truth, for we would have no image of our destiny, no aim or target toward which to move. The mental images, aims, and ideas which mark the first stage of our understanding are thus very important to us. They provide us with our first glimpse of a complex reality, a reality with many faces. Idealistic images of the Truth are in fact one face of that reality—one face of the real world.

QUESTIONS & ANSWERS

It's hard for me to get a sense of the Middle Way as an aim or target. Can you explain how the Middle Way can work as a guide for our action?

Ancient scriptures usually illustrated Buddhist concepts with similes or metaphors in order to make them more understandable. Perhaps such a device would be helpful in this case. We can think of life as a road or highway. All roads have their destination, but from our vantage point on the road, that destination is usually not visible to us. The scenery on both sides of the road is visible, however, and it is often quite interesting and seductive. There are beautiful mountain vistas, forests, and rivers which draw our eyes away from the road. There are billboards advertising all kinds of wonderful things. Some promote their products as the ultimate in comfort and enjoyment. Others offer instant fame and success, while still others

promise to show us the way to omniscent enlightment or spiritual bliss.

Almost without realizing it, we find ourselves turning the
wheel of the car to the right or left—but the highway of life
has no scenic sideroads. On the side of the road there are only
potholes and dangerous ravines. If we drive the car into a
ditch, it may be a long time before we can get back on the road
again. So the aim of our life is simply to stay on the road. We
should not be overly concerned about our future destiny. The
problem is our safety, here and now. If we feel ourselves being
pulled to the right or the left by fantastic ideas or materialistic impulses, we should correct our course; we should turn
back to the middle of the road.

This is the meaning of the Middle Way as the target of life.
The Middle Way is not a fantastic or seductive target, but a
very practical standard for judging the appropriateness of our
thoughts and actions. It is a standard which keeps us moving in
the right direction. With such a standard, we can enjoy our
drive through life without fear of the illusory sidetracks and
dangerous ravines on either side. If we follow the Middle Way,
we can arrive at the destination of true Buddhism more quickly
than by any other path.

*Is idealism always the first manifestation of the will to the
Truth?*

No, I don't think so. The will to the Truth manifests itself
very simply and directly in childhood. When a child finds a
strange insect, he wants to know its name. When he comes upon
a snake in the field, he strikes at it with a stick. He tries
to find out what it is. Such simple curiosity is a very pure
manifestation of the will to the Truth. When he is older the
same impulse which caused him to ask about the insect draws him
to bookstores and perhaps to Buddhist seminars.

So, all manifestations of the will to the Truth are not idealistic. It just happens that when we begin to study philosophy or religion, the will to the Truth usually appears in the form of idealistic questions and ideas. To have the will to the Truth is our basic character, our fundamental nature as human beings. So we must not lose the will to the Truth...we must not throw it away.

You explained that the will to the Truth is very basic, that all our efforts in life flow from the will to the Truth. If this is so, why is it necessary to establish, nurture, and retain it?

It is because the original will to the Truth, which is shared by all people, may, in fact, be directed toward many aims. Thus, there is the will to fame, the will to profit, the will to power, and so on. Such desires and ambitions are not necessarily bad or unnatural, but they tend to obscure the will to the Truth itself. We become so caught up in our secular endeavors that we cannot see the true aim of life. At some point, however, we may suddenly see the emptiness of our blind rush toward power, fame, or security. We may feel that all our efforts in life have come to naught. It seems that there is nothing more to live for, nothing left on which to base our lives. It is at such moments of despair that the will to the truth may assert itself. This is what it means to establish the will to the Truth. To establish the will to the Truth is to discover the illusory nature of our thoughts and desires. It is to discover the fact that, here and now, we have nothing to rely on—nothing, that is, except the will to the Truth itself.

CAUSE AND EFFECT

A man is born with the will to the Truth. He has the will to know, the will to find out, the will to understand—naturally. As he lives, the will to the Truth may lead him in many directions. If he is sincere and follows his intuition resolutely, he may meet Buddhism. At first he reads about the teachings of Gautama Buddha, and he tries to understand. Perhaps he understands a little; perhaps he understands nothing. At any rate his curiosity is aroused. He reads more books, attends lectures, practices zazen, and continues his efforts to understand. He finds concepts like Buddha-nature, Dharma, and the Middle Way. He would like to understand such concepts. He would like to find the rule of the universe, realize his true Buddha-nature, and live his life according to the Middle Way. And so he begins to work toward those intellectual aims which he has found in the teachings. At first his efforts are very sincere, naive, and idealistic. At the beginning of our search for the Truth, we must be idealists.

But in our efforts to reach the target of Buddhist life, we encounter many annoying difficulties. When we practice zazen, our knees become stiff and painful, our backs tired and sore. Our thoughts wander into all sorts of trivial areas of life, and we can't seem to settle down. It is very irritating that we can't sit comfortably and quietly. The master is silent and serene, but we can't seem to find the right position. It is very irritating, very annoying. How can we find the peace and tranquility of the Middle Way when our knees are on fire?

It may be annoying, but the intrusion of physical realities into the world of our idealistic efforts is very important. Sooner or later we must acknowledge another side of life. We must admit the importance of our physical or material existence. Our life is not only ideals, spirit, or mind. Our life is also muscles, blood, and bones. If we were only spiritual beings, we could live our lives without regard for such intellectually trivial matters as food, shelter, physical comfort and health. But in our real lives, such matters are not trivial at all; they are very important and fundamental. If we miss a meal, we become hungry. If we don't eat for several days, our bodies become weak and thin; we feel tired and sluggish; our thinking ability is impaired. If spirit or mind were the only basis of life, such facts would seem very queer. But such facts are real in our lives. We must acknowldege such facts. We must realize that there is a side of life which cannot be explained in terms of spiritual aims or ideas; that when we look closely at that side of life, we can only conclude that our lives are based in the material world.

This was one of Gautama Buddha's most important discoveries. He found that life cannot be cut from its physical foundation. He saw that life is bound inextricably to the earth, the elements, and the laws of the physical universe. Since Buddha recognized the importance of the physical basis of life, he wanted to understand that basis. So he studied life in its relation to the physical universe. He observed the activity of life on this planet very keenly and precisely. In the course of his research he found that the world in which he was living was an orderly world. It was a world ruled by a stern and unbending law. Not only the physical world, but all aspects of life were bound by this exacting rule. The law which Gautama Buddha discovered was the law of causation: the rule of cause and effect.

CAUSE AND EFFECT

So Gautama Buddha taught us that our lives are ruled by cause and effect, and he explained the situation by way of a kind of model or schema which traced the over-all pattern of cause and effect relations in our lives. The pattern he described followed a sequence of twelve distinct stages. At each stage a new element in the process emerged, and these twelve elements were seen as links in a chain: the twelve-fold chain of cause and effect.

The first element in the chain of cause and effect is the most difficult to define. The idea that all things have a beginning is simple enough, but what is the actual nature of things at the first moment of existence? What are the conditions surrounding the moment of birth? When we look deeply into such problems, we are confronted by enigmas, complexity, and an overriding sense of ambiguity. Being a practical religion, Buddhism accepts this ambiguous character matter-of-factly and suggests that it is a reflection of the real state of all things at the beginning. At the beginning, nothing is clearly defined or distinguished from any other thing. There is no figure or ground, no subject or object, no definite relationships of any kind. What there is is very difficult to grasp or understand except by way of an abstract concept. And so we give a name to that ambiguous state of being at the first moment of existence. We call it *chaos*. Chaos is the first element in the chain of cause and effect. In the midst of chaos, there is movement or *action*. It is action of the simplest kind, undirected action like the moving hands and feet of a newborn baby. Such activity gives rise to simple awareness or *consciousness*. The first three elements—chaos, action, and consciousness—are thus stages in the emergence of mind or the mental side of life.

The development of consciousness brings the suggestion of something outside of consciousness. That something is the *external world*. The external world appears and is defined through the functioning of the *six sense organs*. The touching of the organs of sensation and the external world is known as *contact*. Thus, while the first three factors describe the emergence of mind, the second group of three factors is concerned with the physical side of life, or matter.

The contact between the six sense organs and the external world gives rise to feeling or *perception*. We perceive this as opposed to that, and such discrimination leads to *like and dislike* and the situation of wanting or attachment. To want leads us to reach out for what we want. The *effort to get* or grasp something is the ninth link in the chain of cause and effect. The series beginning with perception and ending with the effort to get what we want can be understood as a third sub-chain in the larger schema of cause and effect. This group of three elements describes the cause-and-effect relationships leading to action. Action usually has an aim or goal as its impetus. Our attachment to the objects of perception leads naturally to action in the world.

Such action has its result. We do get something. We develop a consciousness of *possession* or ownership. Possession refers not only to the ownership of things, but to a fundamental sense of "having" something. We feel that we "have" our bodies. We feel that we "have" our thoughts and ideas, our minds. Such feelings of possession are fundamental to our sense of being. They are the foundation of our day-to-day *life* in the world. Life does not continue forever. It is a process which leads inevitably to the experience of *aging and death*. Death represents the final balancing of accumulated cause and effect relationships. From death the situation returns to the state of unconsciousness, or chaos, and the eternal pattern of life can begin once more. Thus the final three factors in the chain of cause and effect summarize the whole process we call life and reminds us that this process must be viewed as a totality—a totality which is ultimately beyond our capacity to explain. I believe, then, that in its structure, the twelve-fold chain of cause and effect reveals the wider pattern of the four philosophies. Thus, in simplified form we can think of the series of twelve elements reduced to four. They are mind, matter, action, and life itself.

I'm not sure how this theory may appear to you. Perhaps it seems rather primitive or strange. Nowadays, when we talk about cause and effect, it is usually in relation to the natural sciences. Modern science has made the rule of cause and effect a matter of common knowledge, but in the day of Gautama Buddha there were no such exact sciences. Many events in the world appeared to arise through magical or mysterious circumstances, or by chance. Gautama Buddha rejected such notions. He believed that all events in the world arise through the orderly action and interaction of the complex elements of the natural universe. He felt that life itself could be understood as a product of very exact and orderly cause-and-effect relationships, and he tried to illustrate such relationships with the twelve-fold chain of cause and effect.

I think modern science has confirmed Gautama Buddha's opinion. When we study this world with the help of our splendid sciences, we find that it is ruled perfectly by the law of cause and effect. Science thus affirms Buddhist theory and Buddhism affirms science. Buddhism and science are in fact preaching the same theory.

There is, however, an important difference between Buddhism and science. Science generally limits its observations and explanations to the natural world. Gautama Buddha felt no such constraints. He believed that the same exacting rule which brings order to the material universe operates in every other phase of life. Thus, according to Buddhist theory, the law of cause and effect can be found in mental or spiritual matters, in the problems of society and human relations, and even in the realm of morals or ethics. In regard to such matters Gautama Buddha taught a very simple theory. He said that if a man does right, he will become happy. If he does wrong, he will become unhappy. In other words, good cause $\rightarrow$ good effect, bad cause $\rightarrow$ bad effect. So if we want to be happy, we must be good, we must be right. It sounds too simplistic, too straight and uncompromising, but this simple theory contains a truth which can change our lives. If we believe in this theory, we can live our lives bravely, without fear or uncertainty. It is a simple idea—a naive theory—but in our real lives this theory is true.

QUESTIONS & ANSWERS

Do the twelve factors in the chain of cause and effect always arise one by one as you described?

There are two ways of thinking about cause and effect. One way is to observe the action of cause and effect on the line of time, from past to present to future. That kind of linear pattern is easy for us to understand and we can find many examples of cause and effect relationships which follow such a pattern. But Buddhism is concerned primarily with the problem of the here and now, or the moment of the present. When we consider cause and effect at the moment of the present, we must change our point of view and our understanding of cause and effect itself. At the moment of the present, all factors exist simultaneously. The universe is a great mass of factors which are related to each other in complex, yet orderly fashion. Thus, our situation here and now relies on a kind of interlocking system of cause and effect factors. Such a system is rather difficult to visualize, but as Buddhists we believe that such a system is the foundation of the universe itself.

So, in our real lives it is difficult to isolate this particular cause and that particular effect, isn't it?

Yes, it's true. Our lives and the world in which we are living are extremely complicated, so we usually can't find that this is the cause and that is the effect, exactly. The twelve-fold chain of cause and effect is only an outline, only a method of explaining or illustrating the cause and effect relationships in our lives. So we should not expect to find the twelve causal elements or factors in their precise qualities or in an exact order. On the other hand, if we observe our lives and the world very closely and scientifically, we cannot doubt the existence of the rule of cause and effect. We can find it in our own experience. I have lived about sixty years now, and after those sixty years I must believe in the theory of cause and effect. It is very stern. It is very exact.

You said that if we do a good deed, we will be happy. If we do a bad deed, we will be unhappy. That is cause and effect. But how do we define what is a good deed and what is a bad deed? How do we define good and bad?

In Buddhism, the problem is not a matter of definition; it is not a matter of intellect alone, but a problem of the real situation, the total situation. In Buddhism the problem of good and bad is not a problem to be solved in the mind, but a problem to be solved in our real lives. In our real lives, good action is right action; it is action which is appropriate to the real situation. If we want to act appropriately, we must be in tune with the situation; we must be atuned to the rule of the universe itself. In order to come into harmony with the rule of the universe, we must attain a state of balance which reflects that rule. When we practice zazen, we can enter that state of balance; we can enter a state of physical and mental equilibrium which is always in tune with the on-going situation. In other words, the state in zazen becomes the standard of our life. With such a standard, we can find what is right and wrong or what is good and bad, at every moment—intuitively. When we act following the truth of zazen, our actions will be appropriate and right, our actions will be good.

I think there is a very big problem about the word "good." For instance, I hear that Gautama Buddha left his wife and family to find the Truth. Most people would say that was not good. So it seems that our usual understanding of good may not be correct...

Yes, it is true. Good does not always conform to our intellectual notions of what is right or wrong. Gautama Buddha left his
family; but if he had not left his family, he could not have
attained the Truth, and if he had not attained the Truth, we
could not find the salvation of our life through Buddhism. Many
people felt the Gautama Buddha's conduct in regard to his
family was wrong, but that same conduct has been of tremendous
importance and benefit to human beings for thousands of years.
So we cannot judge what is good and what is bad on the basis of
sentiment. There is no absolute standard by which we can say
that such-and-such an action is always good or always bad. We
need a broader standard. The only standard which can fulfill
that requirement is the Truth itself. Good and bad must be
considered from the standpoint of the Truth.

*It seems to me that to base our actions on intuition or, as you
say, to follow the truth of zazen, is a very big responsibil-
ity. If we take action intuitively, people may criticize us.
They may say that our actions are wrong. It takes some courage
to act according to our intuition, doesn't it?*

Yes, at times our actions may be questioned by society. If our
actions are sincere, we need not be concerned about other people's opinions. On the other hand, it might be dangerous to
think that we should act without regard to the realities of the
society in which we are living. Intuitive action following the
truth of zazen is not a matter of obeying every momentary impulse which happens to pop into our minds. Such an idea is
naive and unrealistic. Our state in zazen is balanced and stable, and it leads naturally to action of the same quality. It
is balanced, stable action—action which proceeds calmly in
clear awareness of the situation, the real situation. It is
very realistic action.

*So what should we do if we find ourselves facing a difficult
decision in our lives? Should we obey our intuition or follow
the general rule of our society?*

CAUSE AND EFFECT

Your question reminds me of a story in the *Shōbōgenzō Zuimonki*. The *Shōbōgenzō Zuimonki* is a collection of short talks and comments made by Master Dogen during his teaching career.

One day a young monk told Master Dogen that he had an earnest desire to enter a temple and devote himself fully to the study of Buddhism, but he hesitated to do so because of his obligations to his mother. His mother was very old and depended on him entirely for support. If he entered a temple, he could no longer send her money and she would soon die. What should he do in such a situation?

Master Dogen's answer was very candid and realistic. He said, "That is a very difficult question. Even I cannot answer that question for you. It is your problem and only you can find the right answer, but I feel that there might be a way for you to become a priest and still provide for your mother's health and security. It might be difficult, but if we have a sincere will to do something, a way can usually be found. So I hope you can find such a way. I hope you will be able to support your aged mother and, at the same time, devote yourself to Buddhism by becoming a priest."

So Master Dogen's answer was not idealistic or sentimental. He did not say that the monk should leave his mother. Nor did he say that looking after his mother was the most important task in his life. He simply said that it was a difficult problem, a problem for the young monk to solve for himself, and he suggested that there might be a good solution—a realistic solution. Master Dogen always looked for realistic solutions. He always considered the problems of life on the basis of reality.

Our lives contain many problems. Difficult problems are in fact the substance of our lives. To solve difficult problems is thus our life itself. To solve difficult problems is Buddhist practice itself. When we have a difficult problem, we should look for the best possibility, the most realistic possibility. Looking for such possibilities is Buddhist practice itself.

"NOT TO DO WRONG"

I would like to continue our discussion of right and wrong. I think it is a very important problem. I think the problem of what to do in our lives is the central problem of philosophy, religion, and of life itself. Most religions regard morality as a matter of obeying the moral law of god. It is thus a spiritual problem, a problem of conscience, a problem of good thought versus bad thought. Buddhism takes a very different view of the problem. Morality, from the Buddhist standpoint, is not a matter of right thought, but of right action. Right and wrong are not decided in the mind, but in the real world. The Buddhist attitude toward moral problems is thus not spiritual or idealistic. It is very practical and down to earth. Such a practical attitude may disturb some people who feel that questions of moral action must be resolved in the mind, but in the mind morality has no substance or reality. It is only in the real world of action that morality itself becomes real. We may think countless good and pious thoughts, but if our actions are not right, such thinking is absolutely useless. This attitude may seem rather harsh, but I think we need such an attitude if we are to learn how to live.

Master Dogen expressed the Buddhist attitude toward morality in many ways. One volume of the *Shōbōgenzō* is titled, "Not To Do Wrong." It begins with these words: "Gautama Buddha said,

'Not to do wrong—to do right—makes the mind pure. This is the teaching of all the Buddhas.'" The emphasis in these sentences is on doing. Not to *do* wrong. To *do* right. Later in the same volume, there is a story about a man named Hakurakuten. He was a famous poet who studied Buddhism under Master Dorin of Choka. One day he asked his Master, "What is the essence of the Buddhist teachings?" Master Dorin replied, "Not to do wrong. To do right." Hakurakuten was astonished by the simple answer. He said, "Even a child of three knows that!" Then Master Dorin replied, "Yes, a child of three may know it, but even a man of eighty cannot practice it." Here again we find the emphasis on doing as opposed to thinking. From the Buddhist point of view, thinking about right and wrong is utterly different form practicing right and wrong. To think is only exercise for the brain. To practice right and wrong is our life itself.

This attitude becomes very interesting when we consider the precepts. The precepts are rules for behavior. They tell us what to do and what not to do. If knowing and doing are so different, what are we to think of the precepts? Can intellectual standards guide our actions? This is an important question. To understand the Buddhist answer, we should first of all know what the precepts are. We should study their concrete qualities and consider their practicality in our daily lives. Then we will be able to understand the relation between Buddhist morality and the precepts and thereby find the true meaning of the precepts in our lives.

To understand the precepts we should remember their origin. As I explained before, when Gautama Buddha lived in India, he had many disciples. They studied the teachings of their Master and practiced zazen diligently. Many among them attained the Truth and became masters themselves. In this way the Buddhist teachings spread quickly. People gathered around the masters to study and practice and to live their lives according to the teachings. They formed the Buddhist order: the Sangha.

When people live together in one place, many problems naturally arise. The Sangha was not an exception to this rule. It was a kind of community, and, as in other communities, some rules were needed to regulate the conduct of its members. Gautama Buddha recognized this fact, so he gave advice to his disciples about how to live correctly. He taught them many rules or standards by which to judge their actions, and those rules eventually became the precepts.

As the Sangha grew and spread through the world, many diverse and complicated situations were encountered. Efforts were made to construct rules for those varied situations, but these efforts created a new problem. It seems that in trying to have a rule for every situation, they soon had more rules than they could remember; the more rules they had, the more difficult it became to act freely. In the years following Gautama Buddha's death, the number of rules increased so much that at one point there were 250 rules for monks and 350 for nuns.

This situation was, in part, responsible for the emergence of Mahayana Buddhism. Many priests and lay followers felt that the excessive reliance on rules and precepts had stifled the original spirit of Gautama Buddha's teachings, and so, about 400 years after his death, they broke away from the order of the elders and established a new order. In that order, the ideal of the Bodhisattva became very important. A Bodhisattva is a person who recognizes the Truth of Buddhism intuitively and devotes himself to its realization within the context of his usual life. In such a life, rules for conduct had to be rather broad and flexible in order to be workable. So the great mass of rules and regulations which had accumulated were summarized into sixteen fundamental precepts. Those sixteen precepts became known as the Bodhisattva precepts; receiving them became the entry way to the Buddhist life of action in the world.

The sixteen precepts are divided into three groups: the three devotions, the three universal precepts, and the ten fundamental precepts. The three devotions are devotion to Buddha, Dharma, and Sangha. Buddha refers, first of all, to Gautama

Buddha. As Buddhists, we feel tremendous devotion to the man
who attained the Truth 2,500 years ago, who established the
Truth as a religion, and who taught his followers the method to
find the same Truth in their lives. The Truth has been realized
by many people since his time. They were all Buddhas. They all
found the Truth through their own efforts. They passed the
Buddhist teachings down through the centuries to our own time.
We are very grateful to them. When we devote ourselves to
Buddha, we are devoting ourselves to all the Buddhas of the
past, the present, and those yet to come: the Buddhas of the
three times.

Devotion to Dharma is devotion to the universe itself. The
universe has its order, its beauty, its laws. As Buddhists, we
seek to enter into the order of the universe itself. We devote
ourselves to that order. We devote ourselves to the rule of the
universe. We devote ourselves to Dharma. Devotion to Dharma is
the foundation of Buddhism.

Devotion to Sangha is devotion to the monks, nuns, laymen, and
laywomen of the Buddhist order. Gautama Buddha taught us to
honor our companions in this Buddhist life. He taught us to
devote ourselves to the community, or society, of those who are
seeking the Truth.

The second group of precepts are the three universal precepts.
The first is the observance of rules. Every society has its
rules. If we fail to follow the rules of our society our lives
will be disturbed. So as Buddhists we should observe the rules
of society.

The second universal precept is called the observance of Dharma. Dharma means the order or rule of the universe. To observe
the rule of the universe is to act appropriately in all situations. It is, quite simply, to do right and not to do wrong.
Thus, the observance of Dharma could be called the observance
of morality. There are many social rules, but we need to follow a morality which transcends the social situation. We need

to follow a morality based on the order of the universe itself.

To work for the salvation of all living beings is the third universal precept. Buddhism teaches us that we are part of the universe. We are not isolated entities, but elements of a grand system which is reflected in every small part, in every being. This means that all beings in the universe share a certain quality or essential nature, a nature which cannot be named or described. So if we are to express our true nature as human beings, it is natural for us to care for that which we have in common with all living beings. It is natural for us to work for the salvation of all living beings.

The devotions and the universal precepts are very wide and inclusive, but perhaps they are too abstract. So there are ten more precepts, which are also condensed or summarized, but which have a very concrete nature. They are the ten fundamental precepts.

No. 1: Don't destroy life. We all have life. Life permeates the universe. In a sense, it is the universe itself. To destroy life is thus to destroy a part of the universe, a part of ourselves. We should not destroy that of which we are a part. We should not destroy life.

No. 2: Don't steal. We have our own places in the world, our own positions and property. So we should not take that which belongs to another. We should not steal.

No. 3: Don't desire to excess. We all have desire. Desire is an important factor in our lives. But excessive desire is not the origin of happiness. It destroys our composure and makes our lives unhappy. So we should recognize the existence of desire, but we should not allow it to rule our lives. We should not desire to excess.

No. 4: Don't lie. We are living in the universe. The universe is the Truth itself. Truth and honesty are bound together. If we are not honest, we can never find our true situation in the universe. So if we want to find the Truth, we must be honest. We must not lie.

No. 5: Don't live by selling liquor. Alcohol tends to destroy the balance of the body and mind. To sell alcohol to others may cause them to lose their way. So we should not take our livelihood from the selling of liquor or other things which may cause harm to others in this world. (I have some doubts about the form of this precept. I feel that the original precept might have been not to drink liquor. Perhaps as Buddhism spread from India to countries like China and Japan, this precept was altered to suit local conditions. In those northern countries, alcohol was considered an important aid to survival during the cold winter months. So, I personally feel that it is important not to drink, but we should recognize the precept in the form it has come to us from the past.)

No. 6: Don't discuss failures of Buddhist priests and laymen. As Buddhists, we try our best to live and practice the Buddhist life. In doing so we often make mistakes. It may sound strange, but our mistakes come directly from our efforts to do our best. This is a simple fact of life. So when we see the mistakes of others, we should not be critical, for their mistakes are only a product of their efforts in this life.

No. 7: Don't praise yourself or berate others. Modern psychology tells us that most of us have some sort of superiority or inferiority complex. Because of these personal tendencies, we are inclined to praise or criticize ourselves and other people. But we are all human beings. If we recognize this simple fact, it is impossible to berate others for their faults, and praising ourselves becomes a waste of breath.

No. 8: Don't begrudge the sharing of Buddhist teachings and other things, but give them freely. Our tendency is to want more than we have. We want more teachings. We want more things. But when we see our situation clearly, we realize that we are part of the wide and glorious universe. We have everything we need already. In such a situation, it is natural to give. We want to share the teachings and our wealth with others. We should do so; we should give freely and unself-consciously, knowing it is a natural activity of our true situation.

No. 9: Don't become angry. Many of us are prone to become angry. Although it may seem a natural part of our character, anger is not our natural state; it is not our natural condition. In Buddhism we seek to find and maintain our composure. Violent emotions tend to destroy that composure; they upset the natural balance of the body and mind. We should not forget this fact. We should not become angry.

No. 10: Don't abuse the three supreme values. Buddha, Dharma, and Sangha are the foundations of Buddhist life. We must honor them, esteem them, and devote ourselves to them.

Listing the precepts in this way is rather dry and tedious. The Buddhist precepts are not philosophically exciting. They are very simple and straightforward. In this, I think they reflect the fundamental nature of the Buddhist religion. Buddhism is a very practical religion. It is concerned with finding the right way to live. Unfortunately, it is not an easy task. We are inclined to make many mistakes and to suffer the consequences. The precepts were created to help us avoid such mistakes. They have been likened to a fence surrounding a wide, beautiful meadow. We are the cows in that meadow. As long as we stay within the fence, our lives are safe and serene, and we can play freely. But when we step outside the fence, we find ourselves on shaky ground. We have entered a dangerous situation. We should return to the pasture. Thus, we can say that the purpose of the precepts is to help us live happy lives.

There is still a problem, however. We need to ask ourselves if the precepts can actually fulfill their purpose. Can the precepts actually guide our actions in the world? Are they really practical? The answer seems to lie, not in the precepts themselves, but in our attitude toward them. If the precepts are to be practical, our attitude toward them must also be practical. This means that we should not regard the observance of the precepts as the primary aim of life. Perhaps this sounds a little strange, but it is the fact in Buddhism. Master Dogen said:

> Even though we should follow the precepts and maintain our purity, it is wrong for us to establish such efforts as the means of attaining the Truth. We observe the precepts because to do so is the proper attitude of Buddhist monks and the usual custom of disciples of Gautama Buddha. Of course, it is very nice to observe the precepts and maintain our purity, but we should not think of such conduct as the fundamental aim of our life.

Perhaps this attitude seems a little too pragmatic or compromising. Most religions take a much less flexible stand. To disobey the precepts is a sin. A sin is a crime against God. Therefore, to observe the precepts is of paramount importance. By comparison, the Buddhist attitude may seem equivocal or weak. To be pragmatic may make our lives more comfortable, but is it really the role of religion to be pragmatic? Buddhism insists that such a realistic attitude is absolutely necessary. Our lives are tremendously complex and varied. If we try to apply the precepts too strictly, we may lose our freedom to act. We are living here and now, so we must find rules which can be used here and now. We must find our precepts at every moment. Reality is changeable so our rules must also be changeable or flexible. True rules must work in the real world. True precepts are changeable and, at the same time, unchanging. This is the nature of the Buddhist precepts. They help us to live correctly. They provide a framework which is exact and rather narrow, and yet we are free to act in the moment-to-moment situations of our lives.

A Chinese priest once said, "No rule is our rule." This statement expresses the Buddhist attitude precisely. The precepts are valuable to us. They can help us before and after we act,

"NOT TO DO WRONG"

but at the moment of the present, we cannot rely on any rule. We must make our decisions directly. At the moment of the present, to be without precepts is our precept. "No rule is our rule."

QUESTIONS & ANSWERS

I am still confused about the relationship between the precepts and real life. If we can't rely on the precepts at the moment of the present, how can we hope to obey the precepts at all?

I'm afraid we can't. Trying to obey the precepts is a hopeless task. The harder we try the more difficult it becomes. Gautama Buddha, Master Dogen, and the great patriarchs of the past all gave up trying to obey the precepts. This sounds strange, but it is true. They found that they could not obey the precepts through their conscious efforts, so they worked on the problem from another angle. They found that when they practiced zazen every day, their lives became simple and clear. They found, in fact, that they could not disobey the precepts.

In our lives, we must make our decisions from moment to moment. They are instantaneous. They are thus dependent on the condition of our bodies and minds at the moment of the present. Therefore, when our bodies and minds are balanced and composed, our actions reflect our composure. When we are "right," our actions will also be right. So the only way to obey the precepts is to change our bodies and minds through the practice of zazen. When we practice zazen, we resume our original nature— our Buddha nature. We are in harmony with the universe at every moment. In such a state, it is impossible for us to break the precepts. When we practice zazen, we become persons who cannot disobey the precepts.

You mentioned that the moral code in most religions is based on the word of God. What is the basis of the Buddhist moral code?

TO MEET THE REAL DRAGON

The basis of Buddhist morality is reality itself. It is the
order of the universe. It is the facts of life which are facing
us at every moment. For a Buddhist the most important thing is
to see those facts very clearly and precisely. It is to see the
real situation, as it is. Buddhist morality is *there*—in the
situation itself. In other words, Buddhist morality has no
basis other than Buddhist morality itself. To understand this
point, we must realize that morality is not a theoretical or
intellectual problem. Morality is a practical problem, a *real*
problem. What to do here and now is the problem, and the answer
is contained in the situation itself. This is the fact, and
facts are the basis of Buddhist morality.

*You said that receiving the Bodhisattva precepts became the
entryway into the Buddhist life. What does receiving the precepts mean?*

To receive the precepts means to formally acknowledge our will
to follow the Buddhist teachings and our decision to become
Buddhists. We "receive" the precepts from our master in a special ceremony to mark that decision.

Could you describe the ceremony?

Yes, it is a simple ceremony. At the beginning, the receiver
speaks of the fleeting nature of life and of his desire to
receive the great precepts of Gautama Buddha. Then the master
reads each precept loudly and asks the receiver if he can keep
the precept. He asks the same question three times, and the
receiver must answer "Yes I can" each time. After the precepts
have been given, the receiver sits in the place of the master,
and the master praises the act of receiving the precepts, saying that a person who receives the precepts enters the state of
Gautama Buddha at once; he stands at the same level as Buddha;
he is a son of Buddha. Thus the receiver becomes a Buddhist and
a disciple of his master.

So, it is a simple ceremony, but I think it is a very important one. Our lives are defined and given form by our actions. If we decide to follow the Buddhist teachings, we should mark that decision formally. The ceremony fulfills that requirement. It makes our decision real and thus imparts a certain power that would be lacking otherwise. To be sincere Buddhists in our thoughts is fine, but we need to express that sincerity in our actions. Buddhism is not only theory, but something real, something active. So if we want to study Buddhism, we should do something. To practice zazen is "doing something." To receive the precepts is also "doing something." Through such actions, we can realize Buddhist Truth. Through such actions, we can become real Buddhists. When we receive the precepts, we can begin a life of action; we can begin our Buddhist life.

I understand that Buddhism has a practical attitude toward morality and the precepts, but if we really doubt our ability to keep the precepts, what should we do? Should we put off becoming a Buddhist until we feel more confident?

If we have the sincere will or desire to observe the precepts, we need not question our ability to do so. To observe the precepts is very important, but to disobey the precepts is not an eternal sin. It is only an effect of some concrete situation in our lives. In our long lives there are bound to be many such situations. As Buddhists we recognize that fact calmly, and at the same time affirm our intention to keep the precepts throughout our lives. This is our way. We receive the precepts sincerely, recognizing their value and purpose in our lives. We esteem the precepts, but we don't worry about them. This was Master Dogen's theory. It is our way.

ACTION:

THE CENTER OF BUDDHIST THEORY

I think the discussions in the last few chapters have skirted a very fundamental issue which we should look at directly. That is the problem of human freedom. Gautama Buddha taught us to observe the precepts. He taught us to do right and not to do wrong. Such teachings seem to presuppose the freedom of human beings. If we are to do right, we must be free. But Gautama Buddha also taught us about the rule of cause and effect. He taught us to see how things actually come about in this world. Nothing arises independently. All things are related and inter-dependent. Our lives and the universe itself are produced through myriad chains of cause and effect reactions. As those chains evolve, expand, and intersect, an interlocking web of causal relations is created; a web in which the universe itself is bound. In such a universe, how can freedom exist?

This is a great problem, a great dilemma. We feel in our hearts that we must be free, but when we look at the evidence of our lives and the world around us, we must wonder. Can it be that freedom is only an illusion? In the Western world, the problem of human freedom rests at the very center of philosophical questioning and debate. For thousands of years, great philoso-phers have wrestled with the conflict between free will and determinism.

TO MEET THE REAL DRAGON

Religious leaders and other idealistic thinkers usually insist that man is inherently free. They see him as the master of his own fate. His choices and decisions are the determinants of his life. He can choose between good and evil, right and wrong, spiritual awakening or material emptiness. The body may be subject to certain physical laws, but the mind or spirit is eternally free. It must be so—or so they believe.

Materialistic philosophers tend to see the idea of human freedom as a kind of wishful thinking. Man is not really free. His actions, his life, and even his thoughts are determined by his genes, his family, his education, and his society. The movement of human history is only the unfolding of cause and effect. Freedom is just an illusion.

Philosophers on both sides of the issue have created elegant theories in support of their points of view. They urge us to take sides—to see the "truth." But many of us would prefer not to take sides. We sense that the choice is too fundamental and far reaching. If we accept the teachings of idealistic philosophers, we must doubt the explanations of science and the reliability of our own senses. On the other hand, if we embrace materialistic philosophy and believe in the rule of cause and effect, we must deny human freedom and the possibility of moral action. It is a hard choice. We would like to find a compromise, a way out of the dilemma, but in fact, there is no way out. We must face the issue squarely. The fact is that we cannot really believe in freedom and cause and effect at the same time. They are utterly incompatible beliefs.

Many philosophers have glimpsed, or believe they have glimpsed, a truth which lies behind such irreconcilable choices and beliefs. Tracing the source of the dilemma to the fundamental division between the subject and the object, they have explored the complex interactions between the two. By a process of logical reasoning called the dialectic, they have moved from one perspective to another and back again, finding in the process that one viewpoint tends to cancel or negate the other, while at the same time being dependent on it. In the midst of such paradoxical relations and interactions, they have found the existence of a third point, a point of contact or juncture, a point where the subject and object must meet. In recognizing the existence of such a point, they have found an apparent alternative to the dogmatic viewpoints of ordinary dualistic thought. By using that alternative viewpoint or mode of thinking, they have been able to move away from the realm of fixed opposites to a more fluid and unified conception of reality: a monistic conception in which the divided worlds of the subject and the object are synthesized into a vision of wholeness or completeness, a vision of oneness.

Unfortunately, such a vision is only a vision, a kind of image. Dialectic thinking is just that: a kind of thinking; it is confined to the realm of the intellect. In the realm of the intellect, it is quite impossible to actually get out of the dualistic world. Thus the philosophers who have used the dialectic have rarely been able to transcend their own innate bias.

The great philosopher, Hegel, used the dialectic to sum up more than a thousand years of idealistic Western thought. He created a model of man and the universe which saw mind or spirit as the underlying basis of all things.

Philosophers like Marx confirmed dialectical reasoning but scoffed at the idea of mind as the foundation of the universe. They argued that all things were manifestations of matter and energy which had evolved to their present form through the inexorable working of the law of causation.

And so the debate has continued, the arguments becoming ever more subtle and refined, and yet the fundamental conflict still remains. No one has found the dialectic to cure the division in the mind and body of man. We are still confused about the most fundamental questions of life; the resolution of basic philosophical problems like the conflict between freedom and cause and effect continues to elude us.

TO MEET THE REAL DRAGON

If great philosophers have been unable to solve such problems, what hope have we of finding the Truth? In fact, I think the Truth is available to all of us in the teachings of Gautama Buddha. He lived in a simpler time. Philosophical thought was not so advanced or refined, but the real problems he faced in his life were not fundamentally different from those we face every day. He was a sincere man who tried to resolve the conflicts which divided his mind and heart. He was well aware of the problem of freedom. He spent long years seeking the perfect freedom promised by religious thinkers, but it always eluded him. He could not escape the weight of his past actions, and he could not ignore the effects of real facts in his life.

So the central problem of Western philosophical history was also the central problem of Gautama Buddha's life. Was the mind or spirit, which leads man to question and seek fulfillment, really the supreme power in the universe? Or was man in fact bound forever by the material laws of cause and effect? Buddha struggled with this problem for a long time. His efforts to resolve the internal conflicts of his life led him away from the dry realms of purely philosophical debate, through a period of materialistic experimentation and indulgence, and finally into a life of simple activities—a life of pure work or pure action. It was in such a life that he found the resolution of the problem which still plagues us in the modern world. Gautama Buddha's resolution of the problem of human freedom came directly from his own experience, so his theory was very simple and direct, yet very profound. If we can understand how Gautama Buddha resolved the conflict between freedom and cause and effect, I think we will be well on the way to understanding the central core of Buddhist theory itself.

So what was his solution? As I said before, Gautama Buddha was a sincere man, so he was very concerned about what to do in his life. Problems of what to do in life are moral problems. When he considered such problems, he found that time was very important. When he thought about his actions in the past, he saw that they were sometimes wrong. He regretted the wrongs he had committed, but he realized that his regret did not really alter the situation. He could not change those actions. He could never return to the past to correct his mistakes. It was rather depressing.

When Buddha turned his attention to the future, he was aware of a different feeling. The possibility of doing good in the future seemed very real. As he lived, however, he came to distrust such hopeful feelings. He found that they were usually based on dreams or illusions. He had many hopes and plans, but he realized that such dreams could never be realized in the future, for the future was just an idea. It was something that existed only in his mind. It had no substance or reality. He could never live in the future.

Finally, Gautama Buddha realized that in the realm of time, only the present moment was real. He could think about his life stretching from the past and into the future, but he could live only at the moment of the present. This was true, not only for him, but for all people and all things; in fact, everything in the universe could exist only at the moment of the present. So Gautama Buddha studied the moment. He studied real time: the time that actually existed. He studied his real life as it appeared moment after moment. He found that thinking and feeling took him away from the reality of the moment. It was only in the midst of activity that the past and future fell away and the clear state of being in the moment appeared. In such a state, he could experience time as it was. What he experienced was simply *now*. *Now*. *Now*. *Now*. Each moment was unique and fully formed. Each moment stood alone in independent dignity, clearly cut from the past, clearly cut from the future. But the moment was a very short time—too short for the mind to grasp. It was just a flash, an instantaneous flash of something. That instantaneous flash was, in fact, everything. It was his life. It was the universe itself.

So Gautama Buddha found that the universe in which we are living is instantaneous, and that discovery gave him a new way of

seeing and thinking about his life and the philosophical problems which had troubled him in the past. He developed a theory
which we might call the theory of the instantaneous universe
or simply the theory of instantaneousness. According to that
theory, time is like a flash of light. When the light flashes,
we and the universe appear. When the light vanishes, we and the
universe also vanish. Our lives are just a long series of such
flashes: a constant appearance and disappearance of life, the
universe, and ourselves. Such a theory is radically different
from our usual conception of time. We usually think of time as
a solid line stretching from the distant past to the future.
But such an understanding is only a mental construction, an
interpretation based on memories and dreams. Such a mental
interpretation naturally emphasizes the past and the future but
neglects the moment of the present, because this moment, here
and now, is beyond reflection; it cannot be grasped by the
mind. So the mind plays with what it can, constantly flitting
from past to future, constantly diverting our attention from
the time which is real. In fact we live much of our lives ab-
sorbed in a mental world of dreams and memories. Dwelling now
in the past, now in the future, we are lost in a world of constantly changing viewpoints, a world of confusion and conflict.
Philosophical doubts are an inevitable part of such a world. We
search for truth in patterns of past chains of cause and effect
or dream of freedom and happiness in the days to come. We
wonder what is real: body or mind, matter or spirit, freedom or
determinism. What is the real meaning of life? What is the
Truth?

For many years Gautama Buddha lived in the same confused world.
He had his own dreams and memories, his own painful doubts and
philosophical questions. His life was based on assumptions
similar to our own, and he made strenuous efforts to resolve
the conflicts which those assumptions created in his life. At
some point, however, he began to relax and live in a simpler
way. He discovered the joy of practicing zazen, and, through
the practice, he entered a naturally balanced state of clarity
and peace. In that state of natural balance, he experienced

time as it was; he perceived and understood the real nature of time, and that understanding completely overturned his former assumptions about his life and the universe. He realized that there was, in fact, no conflict between freedom and cause and effect. In the moment of the present, he was free: free to choose or select his course, free to act or not to act. But the moment itself did not appear by magic. It could only appear as a result of the long series of moments which flashed into existence, one by one, in the past. Thus the past had created the possibility of his life, here and now, and the present moment, here and now, carried the weight of the past. When Buddha thought about the relation between this moment and the past, he could always find the rule of cause and effect; but in his real life, here and now, he was free, utterly free. His life was thus bound by the past and at the same time free. This was Gautama Buddha's resolution of the conflict between freedom and cause and effect. In the moment of the present, we are both free and bound. It is a strange paradox, but it is the case in our lives.

The theory of time, or the theory of instantaneousness, is a part of the wider theory of action in Buddhism. Gautama Buddha explained that life is action here and now. Life and action are thus limited by two factors: time and space. "Here" is the limitation of space. "Now" is the limitation of time. Our real lives cannot exist outside the limits of this concrete place and time. In other words, the situation here and now is our life. Of the two limitations, the most difficult to understand is time, and it is for this reason that the theory of instantaneousness is so important. Master Dogen regarded this theory as the foundation of all Buddhist thought. In his writings, the theory of instantaneouness is always evident in the unfamiliar perspective or standpoint from which he views all problems. It thus appears most often as a kind of attitude which rejects subjective and objective interpretations of reality in favor of a transcendent realism—a realism which sees all things as they exist in the moment here and now. At times, then, the theory is merely implied, but at other times, Master Dogen speaks of instantaneousness directly. One of those passages is found in a chapter of the *Shōbōgenzō* titled: "Awakening the Will to the Truth."

> Generally speaking, the awakening of the will to the Truth and the attaining of the Truth can occur by virtue of the fact that all things arise and vanish in the moment. If this were not true, a wrong once committed could never disappear, and if the wrong did not disappear, good could never reappear in this world.

> Only Gautama Buddha knew the length of a moment precisely. Only he knew that the mind at the moment of the present can produce one word, and one word spoken at the moment of the present expresses one thought. It is said that in the space of time needed for a man to snap his fingers, sixty-five moments pass, and in each moment the five skandas, or aggregates which constitute the universe, both appear and disappear. Ordinary people, while aware of longer units of time, are unable to perceive or conceive of this fact. They are also unaware that in one day and night there are 6,400,099,980 moments, and in each of those moments all things in the universe arise and vanish. It is because of their ignorance of such facts that ordinary people fail to awaken the will to the Truth.

> The profound and fundamental theory of the appearance and disappearance of all things in the moment must be doubted by those who neither know nor believe in the truth of Buddhism, while those who attain the supreme and subtle mind of Gautama Buddha and recognize the essence of Buddhism must inevitably believe in it exactly. These days we have been fortunate enough to encounter the Buddhist teachings, and perhaps it seems that we have understood them, but in fact we believe only in the long moments of time which we can percieve. We may suppose in our minds that Gautama Buddha's theory is true, but the real situation is beyond our intellectual grasp. Therefore, since

the shortest time and the great expanse of 3,000 worlds
are both well beyond our ability to conceive, we should
not be proud of our understanding. It is only through the
power of the Truth as contained in the teachings of Gautama
Buddha that we can look at all living beings and see the
3,000 worlds as they are.

Our lives are passing, moment by moment, even as we move
from this world to the state between life and death, or
from that state to the next life, and this process of constant change continues whether we like it or not. Life and
death can never be stopped, even for a moment, for they
are produced by our actions in the past and not by our
will or intention. Therefore, we should quickly establish
the will to the Truth and the sincere desire to save all
others before we ourselves attain the Truth. For even if
we hold on to our bodies and minds like precious jewels
and refuse to awaken the will to the Truth, we can never
escape birth, old age, sickness, and death. In the final
analysis, life and death are not our own. They pass quickly and are gone.

Master Dogen's words may seem rather harsh and depressing, but,
in fact, his message is very compassionate. He is telling us
the real situation of our lives. He is urging us to wake up and
see things as they are. Of course, it is not easy to throw off
our habitual patterns of thought; it is not easy to transcend
the common-sense view of time. But the Truth has great power.
If we use the power of Gautama Buddha's teachings, we can
change the way we see the world, and we can begin to change the
way we actually live.

We are living at the moment of the present. It is actually a
very simple theory. It is hard to see how such a simple theory
could change our lives, but if we really study this simple
idea, we will find it very difficult to maintain many of our
assumptions about life. The moment of the present is our life,
our reality. The past and the future exist only in our brains.

TO MEET THE REAL DRAGON

The moment of the pressent is *all*. In the moment of the present we can live; we can act. When we act, the distinction between mind and body is lost. When we act, the subject and the external world are combined into oneness. Such are the implications of Gautama Buddha's theory of time. When we begin to see the implications of this theory in our lives, we must utterly change our point of view. Mind and body, spirit and matter, free will and determinism are all dualities based on thought. In the moment of the present, such dualitites cannot exist. There is only this place, this time, this action, this life, this universe—now, now, now.

If we use this theory, we can resolve the conflicts of our great cililization. If we use this theory, we can find the oneness of body and mind, spirit and matter. If we use this theory, we can find the supreme dialectic to synthesize the philosophical conflict between idealism and materialism. And if we make this theory a part of our day-to-day lives, we can live vigorously yet peacefully in the realization that our lives are both free and bound. We can begin a new life, a new life in a new universe.

QUESTIONS & ANSWERS

If time is really constructed as you say, why don't we experience it that way?

I think there is a problem in your question itself. The problem is with the meaning of experience. We have a tendency to confuse our interpretation of experience with the actual experience itself. Our common-sense view of time is one such interpretation. We cannot "experience" the past. We cannot "experience" the future. We can only think about them. By contrast, we cannot really think about the moment of the present. We cannot isolate a moment or observe it in the usual sense. We can only live it or experience it directly. If we are really living fully in the moment, there is really no "time" at all. Time

ACTION: THE CENTER OF BUDDHIST THEORY

exists in thought. The moment exists in reality.

I find it helpful to understand the relationship between our usual conception of time and Gautama Buddha's theory by remembering the definition of a line as it appears in our geometry books. According to that definition, a line is a series of points. Each point is separate and independent, but the arrangement of points, one after another, creates a line. The points, in themselves, are not a line, but seen from a distance they appear as a line. In the same way, the moment of the present is not the long line of time, but when many moments are contemplated in the intellect, they create the impression or appearance of a line: the long and seemingly continuous line of our common-sense notion of time.

So, when we are aware of time, we are in fact thinking, and when we are living or experiencing time directly, we are acting. Unfortunately, we tend to spend more time thinking than acting simply and directly. We are too busy, too mentally active to see what is really happening. There are no quiet spaces in our lives. We are always filling in the gaps with mental chatter. I think this is the reason our intellectual interpretation of time seems so real. We have lost our ability to distinguish between the mental world and the real world. We need to regain that ability. We need to make some space in our lives so that we can find the meaning of direct experience again. We need to come back to the real world—the world of the moment, here and now.

It is still difficult for me to think of time as separate units or moments. When we are moving or acting, our actions appear very fluid and continuous. The Buddhist theory seems contrary to such simple observations of life.

When we watch a movie, we see figures moving very naturally and smoothly on the screen. It never occurs to us that what we are observing is actually a series of individual images, but of course, that is exactly what it is. A movie film is a long strip divided into frames. Each frame is a complete and separate image with no direct connection to preceeding or following images, yet when the film moves rapidly through the projector, the gaps between the frames are obscured and we view scenes in which movement appears very natural and fluid. So the Buddhist theory of time is not really contradicted by our sensory impressions of the world. We must remember that the moments of our lives are very short and fast moving. As they flash and vanish, our lives move on very smoothly and fluidly, moment by moment by moment.

Compared to the speed with which moments come and go, we seem to be rather dull and slow-moving creatures. It is difficult to see how we can act freely in the space of a single moment.

I think scientists who study the brain and nervous system might dispute your characterization. It seems that neural impulses are transmitted through the body with phenomenal speed. In any case, we should realize that what we usually perceive as a single action is actually a complex series of many actions. Each of these constituent actions occurs at a particular moment in time, and in most cases, there is an element of choice involved: some kind of decision to do or not to do has to be made. These "decisions" are not usually of a conscious or intellectual nature. They are very primitive, spontaneous, and direct. They are like a baseball player's "decision" to check his swing, or a photographer's "decision" to snap the shutter at a certain moment. We make countless decisions of this kind every day, and it is these simple and direct decisions which determine the course of our lives.

Of course one action tends to lead to certain other actions as we follow the familiar patterns of our customs and habits. It is in this sense that we are "bound" by the past and the ongoing process of cause and effect. This is also why it often appears that we have no choice, that we have no control over our lives. But, in fact, we do have the power to choose. Each moment of existence provides us with the opportunity to choose our way. We can control our destiny at the moment of the present.

I like to say that our freedom at the moment of the present is like a pearl on a razor blade. It is a strange image perhaps, but please imagine a razor blade. Now place a pearl on the edge of the blade and hold it there with your finger. If you take your finger away, which way will the pearl fall? We cannot predict, can we? The outcome could be determined by the slightest of breezes, the lightest touch of a finger. I think a person's life at the moment of the present is like the pearl on the razor blade. It is very changeable, very unpredictable. Its destiny can be altered at any moment by the slightest push of the will. This is the power of decision at the moment of the present. At the moment of the present we really are free: free to choose, free to act, free to find our own way in a complicated world.

According to the theory of instantaneousness, the present is the only time which is real, isn't it?

Yes...Yes.

So the future is only an idea or illusion?

Yes...

And the past is also a concept?

Yes, in a certain sense, it's true.

So the rule of cause and effect is also unreal, isn't it?

Well, we might say so, but if we do we should be very clear about what we mean by unreal. From the Buddhist standpoint, cause and effect is not something which actually, physically exists, like some kind of power or electricity. Rather, we regard it as a kind of theory or interpretation. We esteem the theory as a very useful tool in understanding our lives, and we accept the theories of scientists and others who base their hypotheses on a belief in cause and effect, but at the same time, we are careful to remember that cause and effect is itself a kind of hypothesis. We can never confirm or certify the existence of cause and effect in our real lives. This is because our real lives exist only at the moment of the present, and at the moment of the present, we have no time to look for cause and effect, no time to consider it. Our real lives are just action—action here and now.

So, your question really brings us back to the problem we have discussed so many times before. That is the problem of point of view. If we look at life as an idealist, the universe is something eternal and unlimited. Mind is the basis of reality; the realities of the mind may or may not conform to the laws of cause and effect. We can be free at any time and at all times: in the present, in the future, even in the past.

The materialistic person, on the other hand, always studies facts objectively and scientifically. For him, all things are finite and bound by cause and effect. He sees science as his ally in his beliefs, and he refuses to consider such unscientific problems as moral choice or human freedom.

For a Buddhist, the viewpoints of the idealist and the materialist are both wrong, or at best incomplete. He is not seduced by the unanswerable riddles of eternity, nor is he discouraged by the sometimes grim facts of existence on this earth. The problems and ideas which consume the attention of his idealistic and materialistic companions do not distract him from his real concern. That concern is his real life as it appears in the moment of the present. In the moment of the present, he can act, he can do something. Doing something, here and now, is in fact all he can do. It is his life. It is his reality. So he does act. He chooses to do or not to do, and in making such simple decisions, he finds real freedom in his life.

ACTION: THE CENTER OF BUDDHIST THEORY

A Buddhist does not stop thinking, of course. He makes his plans for the future, and he remembers the past like any other man. The difference is that he is no longer attached to the viewpoints which divide his fellow men. He regards idealism and materialism as important modes of seeing and interpreting the universe, but he refuses to be caught in their dogmatic and biased arguments. He takes a more detached view, a view which sees things in balanced perspective and recognizes the truly important in all situations. So he does not deny cause and effect, nor does he take a fatalistic view of life. He simply strives to do his best, moment by moment, knowing he is both free and bound.

ZAZEN

The chapters of this book have, thus far, been filled with discussions of philosophy. We have talked about many theories and interpretations of reality: about idealism, materialism, and theories of time and action. Such discussions are always interesting. I like to talk about Buddhist theory and to compare Buddhism with Western philosophical thought. When we become engaged in such intellectual endeavors it is easy to lose track of our original purpose or the purpose of philosophy itself. The purpose of philosophy is, of course, to understand our lives. The assumption behind such efforts is usually that, if we can understand our lives, we will be able to live better lives. This assumption is very natural, but it is one we should look at closely. Can philosophy really help us to live better? Can theories change our lives or solve the real problems of our lives?

Before attempting to answer this question, we should think again about the meaning of the theory of action. The central thesis of the theory of action is that real life, or reality, is something utterly different from thought. It is something which appears in the moment of the present and is realized through our efforts, our actions, here and now. Thought is a different realm entirely. It may, like the image in a mirror, have the appearance of reality, but in actuality it is nothing more than an image, a kind of illusion. Thus, the realm of thought and the real world of action must always be separate; they can never touch each other directly. I think the theory of action is somewhat ironic in that it clearly acknowledges the dislocation between itself as theory and the real world it attempts to describe. It states that the world of action can never really be known through purely intellectual study or effort. We can think, analyze, hope and dream, but unless we actually do something, nothing whatever will be changed.

What does this mean in relation to the question about whether or not philosophy can solve the real problems of our lives? I think it means that the answer must be negative: No, theory alone cannot change our lives. By itself, philosophy cannot solve even the simplest problem in the world. We might study philosophy from now till eternity and still know nothing of reality itself. We might study the theory of action until we had discovered and analyzed every possible ramification and still not realize action itself. I think it is terribly important for us to understand this fact. To look to philosophy or intellectual theories for our salvation is to wander in delusion. To study Buddhism with the mind alone is a waste of time, a waste of life itself. If Buddhism is to have value in our real lives, we must discover the Buddhist method of working in the real world directly. We must follow Buddhism into the realm beyond thought, beyond theory and interpretation. We must find the realm in which Buddhism and reality are one. That is the realm of Buddhist practice or Buddhist action. It is the realm of zazen.

Zazen is not a method of thinking about reality. It is not a method of understanding our lives. When we are practicing zazen, we are sitting in reality itself. When we are sitting in reality, we can recognize ourselves. We can see ourselves sitting there in reality, and we can see the external world as it is. Then we can find that the external world is not really "external" at all, but something which includes us and enfolds us. Thus, in zazen we can study the reality which includes ourselves; we can in fact realize reality or become one with reality. When we become one with reality, we are able to follow the rule of reality or the rule of the universe naturally. Gautama Buddha taught us that to follow the rule of the universe is to become happy; it is happiness itself. Thus, we can think of zazen as the way to hapiness, or as the essence of happiness itself. Master Dogen preferred the latter understanding. He said, "Zazen is not training to attain enlightenment. It is just the universal gate to peace and happiness. It is the practice and experience of perfectly realized Truth." For Master Dogen, Buddhism was not complex or difficult. It was simply the practice of zazen. "To practice zazen is Buddhism...Buddhism is to practice zazen." These were his words, his understanding, and his belief. For Master Dogen, zazen was *all* of Buddhism.

Unfortunately, this is not the only understanding of Buddhist practice. Some sects of Buddhism regard practice as a means of attaining enlightenment. They teach that attaining enlightenment is the aim or goal of Buddhist practice. Master Dogen vehemently denied such theories. He insisted that to practice zazen is enlightenment itself. He said that any theory which regards practice as different from enlightenment is a non-Buddhist theory. We should ask ourselves why Master Dogen was so adamant, so uncompromising. What is the big issue here anyway? To find the meaning of this issue, and to understand why Master Dogen felt so strongly about it, we should study his biography once again.

As you may recall, Master Dogen became a priest when he was very young, and his search for the Truth eventually took him to Kennin-ji temple in Kyoto. There he learned the teachings of the Rinzai sect of Zen Buddhism. The Rinzai sect generally promotes zazen as a method of attaining enlightenment. In their temples, zazen usually becomes a very strenuous exercise to try to break through the walls of conventional habit and thinking and thus to experience a transcendent state of freedom or enlightenment. They employ meditative techniques like concentrating on koans or focusing the attention on the breath as a means of achieving their goal. So their practice has a strongly mental or intellectual quality, and they see the mind as both the obstacle and the avenue to the Truth.

Young Master Dogen was immediately attracted to these teachings, and he began to practice diligently in an effort to experience the great enlightenment they promised. However, after nine years of sincere effort, he found that his goal still eluded him. He was still confused about many aspects of Buddhism, and the focal point of his confusion was the meaning and practice of zazen itself. So he went to China in hopes of finding the answer to his problem. He visited many temples, but in most of them the teachings of Master Rinzai were in vogue, so he was unable to find any new interpretation of zazen. This was a big disappointment for the young priest, and he had almost decided to abandon his quest when he heard that a very famous master named Tendo Nyojō had become the master of Keitoku-ji, a temple Master Dogen had visited on his arrival in China. So he returned to the temple to meet the new master and to ask him the meaning of zazen.

Master Nyojō told him not to be concerned about attaining enlightenment. Rather, he should "just sit," and in sitting find the essence of Buddhism itself. This was a new and startling idea for Master Dogen. Master Nyojō did not promote the study of koans in zazen, or the counting of breaths, or other methods of focusing the mind. He stressed the simple activity of "just sitting," and he urged his disciples to find the meaning of practice in practice itself.

At first, Master Dogen could not understand Master Nyojō's teachings exactly, but he felt the intensity of his beliefs and the sincerity of his actions, so he decided to stay at the temple and try to discover the meaning of Master Nyojō's attitude toward zazen. One day he overheard his master encouraging a priest who had dozed off while practicing zazen, "What is the use of sleeping?" he asked. "Zazen is the falling away of body and mind!" These simple words struck Master Dogen very force-

fully. In them he found a new meaning of zazen and a new understanding of Buddhism itself. He understood that by "body and
mind," Master Nyojō meant the consciousness of body and mind.
Thus, the falling away or casting away of body and mind was the
transcendence of the consciousness of body and the consciousness of mind. It was the transcendence of sensual attachments
and mental illusions, or simply the transcendence of the disturbing factors in our lives. So, practicing zazen was a return
to a simple and harmonized state, a balanced state, a state
beyond the opposing fixations of the body and the mind. Such a
state could not be found through exaggerating the consciousness
of either mind or body with techniques of mental or physical
concentration. It could only be found by entering the realm in
which consciousness of body and mind fall away. That is the
realm of action. Through sincere action at the moment of the
present, the state of natural balance could be achieved at
once.

Finally, Master Dogen could understand the meaning of his
Master's attitude toward zazen. Just sitting in quietness was
the realization of the Truth itself. It was enlightenment itself. To sit sincerely in zazen was the realization of the
state beyond body and mind. It was a state which could be
realized at any moment and at every moment—even by the begin-
ner, even by the dull or the uneducated. The state of the Truth
was utterly beyond such relative concerns. Those who wished to
find the Truth in their lives needed only to practice zazen
every day. To practice zazen every day was to live continuously
in the state of the Truth itself.

Perhaps now you can understand why Master Dogen railed against
the idea that practice and enlightenment were different. He had
spent years chasing an ideal, a vague promise of unusual power
or transcendent understanding that would someday strike him
like a bolt of lightning or the sudden opening of a door to the
Truth. All he had to do was find the key to the door. That key
might be found through identification with the breath, in the
solution of a koan, or in the dissolution of all consciousness

through intense concentration on a point above his naval. The methods were many, but the results were scanty and poor. Finally someone told him to forget what he had learned and just study what he was actually doing. Just look into the practice itself, or better yet, don't look—just do it. And so he did. He just sat quietly on his cushion and eventually he discovered that enlightenment had been there, on the cushion, all along. Enlightenment was in the practice itself, not outside of it, not a product or a goal. It was always there...just sitting in quietness was the Truth itself.

When he had understood the real situation, Master Dogen was determined to transmit the correct understanding of zazen to his native land. Thus, from the time he returned to Japan, he proclaimed his simple message again and again: "To practice zazen wholeheartedly is the attainment of the Truth itself. To practice zazen is Buddhism...Buddhism is to practice zazen."

We should think about the meaning of Master Dogen's words very carefully. We should consider the meaning of practice and enlightenment, again and again. Is practice the way to enlightenment or is practice enlightenment itself? Perhaps the question seems academic, a matter of semantics or intellectual interpretation. But the issue here, as Master Dogen understood, is the dividing line between Buddhism and non-Buddhism. If we bring the wrong attitude to our practice, it will cease to be Buddhist practice. If we see practice as a means of attaining enlightenment, enlightenment will become a kind of ideal and our practice will become a kind of idealistic practice. Buddhism is not idealism. Buddhism rejects the notion that enlightenment or happiness can be realized through intellectual effort or understanding. Buddhism states that the Truth is here and the Truth is now. Happiness exists in sincere action at the moment of the present. Enlightenment and practice are, therefore, one and the same. If we want to study true Buddhism, we must retain this understanding. If we want to find true happiness, we must find it in work, in action, in practice, here and now. We must find it in zazen. Zazen is enlightenment itself.

ZAZEN

Zazen is Buddhism itself. Buddhism is zazen.

QUESTIONS & ANSWERS

Are we to understand, then, that enlightenment as taught by the Rinzai sect is a kind of myth or illusion?

No, not necessarily. You see, we might say that there are two kinds of enlightenment. One is a momentary state of body and mind. When we take our seats on zazen cushions, fold our legs, straighten our backs, and devote ourselves wholeheartedly to sitting in quietness, we are, at that moment, in the state of enlightenment itself. Enlightenment is thus a state of body and mind. It is a thoroughly normal state, a state to be realized in the here and now. It is not a peculiar sensation. It is not the experience of some great intellectual breakthrough. It is just the natural state of balanced body and mind, the state of natural balance. Because it is our natural state of existence, it is not particularly dramatic or subjectively observable. We cannot recognize the state of natural balance. We cannot be conscious of enlightenment. To be conscious of enlightenment is, in fact, to be far removed from the state of enlightenment itself. It is the essence of delusion.

So, generally speaking, we cannot "experience" enlightenment. We can only be in the state of enlightenment itself. There is another kind of realization, however, which we can think of as a second kind of enlightenment. To illustrate this second kind of enlightenment, perhaps I should tell you about my own experience. I started practicing zazen when I was a teenager. At first I practiced sporadically, sometimes intensely, sometimes not at all. As a result, my life was rather unsettled, and I could not find harmony or balance from one day to the next. Then, at the urging of Master Kodo Sawaki, I began to practice zazen every day. Gradually, zazen became a very natural part of my life, like eating, sleeping, or going to the office. Then one day—I can't remember what I was doing at the time—I thought to myself, "Why, *this* is enlightenment, isn't it?" That was my experience or realization of enlightenment. It was not dramatic or exciting. It was just a simple recognition or acknowledgement of the perfection of things as they are. Life is good. The universe in its simplicity and complexity alike is very marvelous and beautiful. We are all living in the state of enlightenment. We have been in the state for a long time... from our births...from the eternal past.

The recognition of the perfect universe may be experienced in different ways by different people, and for many, the experience may never be consciously realized. I think this is not so important. The fundamental enlightenment is not the recognition of the state, but the state itself. This is the fact which followers of Master Rinzai's teachings usually fail to understand. By emphasizing and romanticizing the second kind of enlightenment, they lose touch with the fundamental state which is the real basis of Buddhism itself. By making enlightenment the aim of practice, they tend to seek something outside of the practice itself. There is nothing outside the practice. At the moment of the present, the practice includes all things. Practice is the experience and the realization of the Truth itself. Whether or not we consciously recognize this fact is not so important. The important thing is to practice zazen every day. If we practice zazen every day, we can live our whole lives in the state of the Truth.

The idea of enlightenment is very attractive—almost seductive in a sense, isn't it?

Yes, the idea of enlightenment is very seductive. It makes Buddhist theory and practice seem romantic and somehow easy to understand, but I'm afraid it is a false dream. Enlightenment is not an idea...

Yes, I can understand that, intellectually, but it seems that even if we accept Master Dogen's understanding of practice, the idea of enlightenment is still very much in the back of our

ZAZEN

*minds. It is very difficult to get rid of the idea of enlight-
enment, isn't it?*

Yes, it's true. But if you practice zazen every day, sooner or
later you will find that the idea of enlightenment has become
irrelevant and actually rather boring. You will discover that
you need nothing beyond the practice itself, that you need no
enlightenment—and *that* will be your enlightenment. To find
that we need no enlightenment is enlightenment itself. It is
very ironic, but it is true, I think.

*In your talk, you said that in zazen we can recognize ourselves
as we are sitting in reality. The idea of recognition is hard
to understand. What exactly does it mean, "to recognize ourselves"?*

By recognition, I mean a kind of awareness or a situation of
consciousness. Zazen is not a state without consciousness. In
zazen we are aware of ourselves; we are conscious of our existence on the cushion, in front of the wall, in the quiet room.
We are there, and we are aware of the fact; we recognize that
we are sitting, here and now. This is the meaning of recognizing ourselves in zazen.

Is it an intellectual recognition?

Our consciousness in zazen is not only a situation of the mind,
but a kind of feeling which includes the whole body and mind.
It is a situation which is difficult to define with words, so
Master Dogen usually referred to it as "the ineffable state of
zazen." So, to say that we are conscious of ourselves or that
we recognize ourselves in zazen is a kind of explanation. The
real situation cannot be described with words.

*Many books speak of transcending the self or the ego in zazen.
If we are aware of ourselves in zazen, we haven't really transcended the self, have we?*

I think such explanations are very misleading. They give the impression that something called "ego" really exists, and that we must somehow transcend that entity, whatever it might be. But when we are practicing zazen, we can find no ego. *We* are sitting. That is the fact. That is the situation. So in zazen there is no ego and no transcendence. There is only *we* who are sitting, here and now.

Of course, we can say that when we are practicing zazen, we can transcend the self which is separate from the external world, and we can transcend the external world which is separate from us—but again, these are only explanations. We should not take such explanations too literally. In the real situation there is only the momentary fact. There is only our action, here and now. So we say zazen is "just sitting." Just sitting is not an explanation. It is our way of pointing at the real situation which is beyond words. Just sitting is zazen. In just sitting there is no ego. There is no transcendence.

TO MEET THE REAL DRAGON

In the last chapter I gave you my explanation of Master Dogen's theory of zazen. Now I would like to let Master Dogen speak for himself. Among his many works, perhaps the most concise explanation of Buddhist practice is contained in the *Fukan Zazengi*. It was his first work on returning to Japan from China, and it includes the essence of his understanding of both the practical and theoretical aspects of zazen. During his teaching career, he revised the *Fukan Zazengi* many times, finally producing what is known today as the popular edition. The following is my translation of that edition. I hope that you will find in it the true meaning of zazen and the true spirit of Master Dogen's teachings—that his words will inspire you to seek the Real Dragon in your life.

FUKAN ZAZENGI
The Universal Recommendation for Zazen

Fundamentally, the Truth exists everywhere, so how could it be dependent on practice or realization? Since the means of attaining the essence of Buddhism is abundantly present in every place, how can it be necessary to make strenuous efforts in our lives? Furthermore, our lives (in the temple) are far removed from the delusive complica-

tions of secular society, so why should we concern ourselves with teachings which preach the necessity of elim-
inating delusion through cleansing or polishing? Since we
are always living in the state of perfection, of what use
is even the smallest amount of practice? If, however, the
slightest difference should appear (between our real
state and this state of perfection) it will become as
wide as the distance between heaven and earth, and if any
discriminating thoughts of good and bad should arise in
our minds, we will be lost in confusion—unable to decide
what to do. If, for example, we are proud of our understanding and abundant experience and think that we have
attained some part of the Truth or illuminated our minds,
and even if our minds then become so vigorous that we
feel as if we have pierced the heavens and are wandering
in the realm of the enlightened—it is really only our
heads which have entered the sphere of the Truth. In such
a situation, we utterly lack the means of transcending
the intellect and entering the vigorous world of action
with the whole body and mind.

In the opening paragraph, Master Dogen affirms the fundamentally positive and optimistic attitude of Buddhist theory: the
Truth is everywhere. All things and all people are part of the
perfect world, the perfect universe of Dharma. Thus, we are
always living in the state of perfection.

But—he hastens to warn us—there is a difference between the
world of Buddhist theory and the real world as we actually
experience it. In our day-to-day lives we encounter many confusing and contradictory situations. In such situations it is
difficult to act with confidence and composure. We hesitate. We
move too fast or too slowly. We get out of step with the rule
of the universe, and all our efforts seem only to compound and
exaggerate our sense of separation from the balanced and harmo-
ious world of the Truth. In this situation the dualistic perceptions of the intellect are of little value. In fact, the
human tendency to divide and catagorize, to discriminate be-

tween good and bad in all situations, serves only to confuse us and to render us incapable of action.

Many people are unaware of this fact. They cannot recognize the difference between theory and reality, between thought and action. This confusion may lead them to the ultimate delusion: the belief that they have attained enlightenment. Because they do not distinguish between theory and the real world, they think that enlightenment is a matter of knowledge and understanding. They may understand Buddhist theory or believe that they have understood it, but, in fact, they are stuck in the realm of thought: they have entered the realm of the Truth only with their heads. Such people know nothing of the realm of the Truth which includes the whole body and mind. They know nothing of the vigorous world of action.

> Remember that Gautama Buddha practiced zazen for six years even though he was naturally endowed with great wisdom and brilliance; and Master Bodhidharma, who transmitted the Truth at Shao-lin temple, also sat facing the wall for nine years. We can hear their voices even today. If the ancient sages were like that, how is it possible for us not to practice zazen? Therefore, we should cease our efforts to gain the Truth through the study of words and letters. Rather, we should learn the activity which works in the opposite direction, thereby illuminating ourselves in our own reflected light. If we do so, our consciousness of body and mind will fall away naturally, and our original face will appear, here and now. If we want to attain the ineffable, we must practice the ineffable, at once.

Even Gautama Buddha and Master Bodhidharma practiced zazen. So we must follow their example. We must stop trying to find the Truth only through intellectual effort. We must, in fact, work in the opposite direction. Master Dogen believed that our efforts in life can lead us in two directions. Usually we acknowledge only one direction as a positive alternative. We want to make progress, to go forward, to get more or to know more—

onward, ever onward. But Master Dogen felt that if we are to find the Truth, we must actually reverse our direction. We must take a step back. When we are practicing zazen, we are stepping back into a simpler, more primitive state. In zazen we cease trying to get something or hold on to something. In zazen we can lose everything, and when we have lost everything we are "just sitting." Then our original face appears. We expose ourselves to ourselves. We are bathed in our own reflected light. This is not an experience which can be described. The state in zazen is ineffable. To attain the ineffable state, we must simply *do* it. How can we do it? Master Dogen gives very concrete instructions:

> For the practice of zazen, a quiet room is desirable. Food and drink should be taken moderately. Forget trivial circumstances. Set aside worrisome concerns. Don't think of good or bad. Don't consider right or wrong. Stop the restless movement of mind, will, or consciousness. Cease the mental manipulation of images, thoughts, and feelings. Don't try to become Buddha! These efforts need not be confined to the practice of zazen, but should be carried over into the realm of our everyday activities like sitting or lying down.

> We usually place a thick mat on the floor where we sit and put a round cushion on top of that. Then we take the full or half lotus posture. In the full position, place your right foot on your left thigh and your left foot on your right thigh. In the half position, only put your left foot on your right thigh. Arrange your clothing loosely yet neatly. Then put your right hand (palm up) on your left foot and your left hand on your right palm, holding the tips of the thumbs together. Sit upright holding your body straight, inclining neither right nor left, forward nor backward. Hold your head straight so that your ears are equidistant from your shoulders and your nose is in line with your naval. Place your tongue against the roof of your mouth, closing your lips and teeth firmly. Open your

eyes naturally and allow the breath to pass through the nostrils quietly.

After regulating your posture in this way, take a deep breath, swing your body right and left, and begin to sit in the balanced state of non-movement. Consider the state of nonthinking. How can we consider the state of nonthinking? By "not-thinking"! This is the secret of zazen. Zazen is not training to attain enlightenment. It is just the universal gate to peace and happiness. It is the practice and experience of perfectly realized Truth.

In zazen we need not think; we need not feel. We simply sit. We sit with sincerity, with the whole body and mind. Sitting is not thinking, and it is not nonthinking. It is something very direct and simple, something which transcends both thinking and feeling. That something is action. It is "not-thinking." This is the secret of zazen.

In zazen the universe is realized here and now—nothing can disturb or hinder it. If you understand this fact, you will become free and powerful like a dragon which has found water, or a tiger standing before a mountain. Then the true rule of the universe will manifest itself, and passivity and confusion will disappear at once.

In the Orient, dragons and tigers are symbols of power and dignity, but they can have their power only in their natural environment. Dragons draw power from water. A tiger standing in the shadow of a mountain is proud and invincible. When we practice zazen, we gain the power and dignity of our natural state. We become strong—poised to act or not to act as the situation requires. In such a state, the imbalanced conditions of the body and mind which cause us to be either too passive, or too aggressive and confused, both disappear.

When we have finished our practice, we should move slowly and stand up calmly. Our actions should not be violent.

TO MEET THE REAL DRAGON

We can find many examples in the past of masters who completely transcended the difference between ordinary people and saints, or died while sitting or standing up; their power came directly from the practice of zazen. Furthermore, it is impossible for us to understand, with our discriminating intellect, the circumstances in which Buddhist masters were able to express the Truth with finger, pole, needle, or wooden mallet; and the Buddha-state of masters who transmitted the Truth to their disciples with a *Hossu**, fist, staff, or shout of *Katsu*! is equally beyond our grasp. Neither can such matters be understood through mystical powers or a divided view of practice and realization. The state in zazen is clearly something more than mere form or sensory stimuli. How then can we doubt that the state in zazen transcends both intellectual recognition and perception? Therefore, we need not discuss whether we are learned or uneducated, nor divide the clever from the stupid. To practice zazen wholeheartedly is the attainment of the Truth itself. In zazen there is no difference between practice and realization; through its influence, all our actions are performed in the balanced and timeless state.

Buddhist masters have attained marvelous powers through the practice of zazen. Among them, the most important is the transcendence of relativism, the attainment of a state which is beyond dualistic perceptions and interpretations of reality. This is the Buddha-state, the state of oneness with the real world. When the great masters of the past attained this state, all their actions became direct expressions of the Truth. Thus, they often expressed the Truth in unconventional ways. Master Gutei always raised one finger when asked to explain the unexplainable. Bodhisattva Manjusri struck a wood block with a mallet crying, "*This* is the Truth!" Other masters used a *Hossu*, their fist, or a sudden shout to transmit the Truth which exists here and now.

---

*A *Hossu* is a small ceremonial staff with a plume of horsehair.

TO MEET THE REAL DRAGON

The circumstances in which these actions were performed and the transcendent state of the masters themselves will always remain a mystery to us unless we ourselves enter the same state. To do so we need only practice zazen. When we are sitting sincerely in zazen, we can realize the Truth at once, for to act sincerely in the moment is itself the transcendence of duality. Therefore, practice and realization must be one. There can be no separation of practice and realization when we are acting wholeheartedly in the moment of the present.

> Generally speaking, whether in this world or in other worlds, in India or in China, all those who have received the Buddha-mind and utilized it perfectly have practiced zazen and found the binding standard of action in the state of non-movement. So, even though there are a multitude of situations and a variety of ways to study Buddhism, we should devote ourselves solely to zazen and the pursuit of the Truth. What is the use of wandering in distant lands forsaking our own place of practice? If we make a mistake at the first step, the all-important moment of the present will be lost forever.

"Wandering in distant lands" is an allusion to a famous story in the *Lotus Sutra*. It is about the son of a king who lived and wandered outside his father's kingdom, unaware of his true identity or his noble birth. One day he happened to return to his native land. When his father saw him, he recognized his long lost son at once. But the king realized that if he approached the boy directly, he would be frightened and flee from the country again. So he employed his son as a common laborer and then gradually promoted him until he had become his chief minister. At that point, the son had found his normal state. He had regained his normal human mind, so the king could tell him of their true relationship without fear of losing him again.

The meaning of the story is that all human beings have Buddha-nature, but they are usually unaware of the fact. They have wandered in the far countries of delusion so long that they cannot recognize their homeland, even though they are in the midst of it at every moment. If we practice zazen, we can come back to our homeland at once. We may not recognize the fact immediately, but if we continue our efforts for a long time, we will one day realize that we have been "home" all along. We will find that we do indeed have Buddha-nature, that Buddha-nature exists, here and now, at our place of practice, wherever it might be.

> Now we have had the good fortune to be born with the precious human body, so we should not pass even a moment in vain. Since we possess the essential basis for pursuing the Truth as human beings, how can we be satisfied with transient pleasures which fly like sparks from metal and stone? Our bodies are as fragile as dewdrops on the grass, and our lives are like flashes of lightning: they appear in a moment and are gone.

> So my friends who wish to study Buddhism—don't become attached to images of the Dragon, and don't be afraid to meet the Real Dragon in your life. Earnestly strive to attain the Truth which is direct, here and now. Revere those who have transcended Buddhist study and are living life simply—as it is. Meet the Truth of the Buddhas and receive the state of the Patriarchs. If you practice the essence of Buddhism, you will become the essence of Buddhism. Then the doors of the treasure house will open naturally, and you will be free to enjoy its contents as you like.

There was once a man who was fascinated by dragons. The walls of his house were covered with paintings of dragons and every shelf was lined with dragon statues and figurines. In fact his whole house was filled with images of dragons. One day a real dragon happened to look in his window. When it saw all the images of itself, it was overjoyed, for here, clearly, was a man who loved dragons. Surely he would be pleased to have a real dragon visit his house. But when the man looked out the window and saw the dragon, he was so frightened he fainted straight away.

So Master Dogen's advice is very clear. We should not chase after images of the Truth. We should not become attached to theories or intellectual explanations. Rather we should meet the Truth directly. To practice zazen is to meet the Truth of the Buddhas. To practice zazen is to meet the Real Dragon, face to face.

QUESTIONS & ANSWERS

The opening words of the Fukan Zazengi *seem very important to me. Master Dogen said that the Truth exists everywhere and the means of attaining it are present in every situation. Then, as you explained, he went on to talk about the existence of delusion—about the fact that dualistic thinking tends to create a sense of separation between ourselves and the world, and that this, in turn, leads to confusion and suffering. This may be true, but it seems to me that the fundamental problem is not the confusion itself, but our reaction to it. If the Truth exists in every situation, it must exist even in confusion. So a situation which appears totally confusing and unmanageable may, in fact, be perfectly balanced, perfectly OK, as it is. It is our constant efforts to change or manipulate the situation which actually upsets that balance. So as I understand Buddhist theory, our task is simply to let things be, as they are. If we relax and allow events to take their own course, most of our problems will take care of themselves, won't they? There is really no need to make special efforts to change ourselves or our situation, is there?*

I'm afraid such thinking is exactly the kind of intellectual rationalization which Master Dogen was talking about. To think that everything is OK, so there is no need to change anything, or to make an effort to attain our balanced state, is just the sort of misguided thinking we must guard against.

The world is changing at every moment, and we are part of that changing world. We cannot sit back in our easy chairs and observe the sincere efforts of our fellow men as if they were acting in some kind of comic movie or play. We have to get into the movement of life. We have to follow the changing universe of which we are a part. To follow the changing universe is to move with the universe at every moment. It is to keep pace with the continuously changing world. When we are practicing zazen we are doing just that. We are following the universe directly, here and now. So living quietly and sincerely, from moment to moment, is our best life, our natural life, and our efforts to live such a life are our natural efforts: they come from our natural state as human beings.

Unfortunately, we have a tendency to lose that natural state. We have a tendency to think too much. We think and think and think some more. Thinking becomes our life, and we cannot see anything outside the realm of thought. In such a life of think-ing we are inclined to enter the blissful realm of the gods. To wander in the realm of the gods is not our natural state. It is not our original state as human beings. On the other hand, we might follow the opposite tendency and become overly attached to our physical sensations and feelings. To live continuously in the realm of the senses is to live as animals. It is not the balanced state of human beings.

So Gautama Buddha urged us to become real human beings. He urged us to come back to our natural state, our original state. To do so requires some effort. We have to cut the chain of thought deliberately. We have to transcend our attachments to mind and body through sincere action, here and now. So, some simple and direct effort is absolutely necessary. We should not let our intellect blind us to this fact. We should not be mis-led by theories which provide a rationale for inaction or indo-lence. Effort is very important. It is life itself.

TO MEET THE REAL DRAGON

Perhaps there is a need to make some effort in our lives, but I still wonder about the direction those efforts should take. Practicing zazen is an effort which is directed toward the self. How about those efforts which are directed outwardly? Should we try to change the world, or should we allow the world and our own situation in the world to evolve without interference?

I am afraid there is no fixed rule to cover each and every situation. Sometimes it is appropriate and right to try to change the world, and sometimes it is not. We are always bound, to some extent, by the various factors which constitute our situation, so we should not overestimate our ability to change that situation dramatically. Still, there are times when we must try. At those times the decision to act cannot come from intellectual consideration alone, but from an intuitive sense of what the situation really is. That intuitive sense will be right if our bodies and minds are right. When a man is in the state of natural balance, he may, at times, try to change the world, and at other times, he may, in your words, let it be. Both situations are natural for him. We should not try to dictate his response to the real situations of his life.

Master Dogen said the secret of zazen was "not-thinking." What is "not-thinking"?

"Not-thinking," expressed positively, is to do or to act. It means to do something other than think. Most of our life is spent in pursuit of thought or sensation. We rarely have a time when we can devote ourselves to action. When we are practicing zazen, we need not think, we need not feel. We just act. We just sit. "Just sitting" is zazen.

To say that we need not think or feel seems strange to me. When I practice zazen, I find that my thoughts and sensations continue almost as before.

Yes, it's true. The state in zazen is not a state devoid of all thoughts and feelings, but a state in which we gradually cease to chase after thoughts and sensations, actively. When we first sit down on our cushion, our habitual patterns of thinking and feeling continue for some time, but at some point, the chain of thought becomes less solid and continuous. Gaps begin to appear in the stream of consciousness; they gradually become longer and more numerous until, at last, we enter a state of quietness, a state of balance and tranquility. Even then we are not without thoughts and feelings, but the images which appear are very simple and concrete. We may see a spot on the wall or an insect crawling on the floor. We may hear birds singing or feel sharp pains in our legs. Such perceptions have no conceptual or emotional overlays. They are very direct and primitive. They just appear naturally and vanish without a trace.

When we are enjoying such a state, we do not interfere in the natural flow of mental images and perceptions. We make no effort to grasp, repel, or manipulate the images which appear. We cease the active or intentional pursuit of thoughts and sensations. This is what I mean when I say that we need not think and we need not feel.

So we should not be disturbed by our thoughts in zazen?

Yes, that's right.

But when we become aware of our thoughts, they seem to become very heavy, very neurotic. It seems that we cannot control our thoughts.

There is no need to control our thoughts. To try to avoid thinking, or control our thoughts, is really just another kind of thinking. In zazen we should transcend thinking and non-thinking. Just be sincere in your sitting. That is the secret of zazen.

But how can we do that?

By taking care that your spine is straight. It sounds too simple, but that is the essence of our efforts in zazen. We don't need any elaborate methods of focusing the mind or balancing the body. To take the proper posture and maintain it sincerely is to enter the balanced state directly. So when you find that you are thinking, just remember your posture. Is your spine straight? Are you leaning to the right or to the left? Sitting sincerely is just a matter of making such simple adjustments, again and again. Sitting sincerely is "just sitting." That's all. There is no hidden or mystical meaning. It is as simple as it sounds: "just sitting" is simply to sit with the whole body and mind.

How long should we practice?

I usually recommend a period of forty-five minutes in the morning and, if possible, again at night. But at first that may be too long. So just sit as long as you can. Perhaps, at first, that will be only five minutes or ten minutes, but if you practice every day the period will become longer naturally. So, today five minutes, tomorrow ten minutes, and so on, as you can.

What if, during the five or ten minutes, there is only chatter?

We need not discriminate between zazen which is full of chatter and zazen which is quiet and serene. The first five minutes of ceaseless chatter are just as important as the final minutes of quiet serenity. Sometimes zazen is quiet. Sometimes zazen is noisy. Both situations are fundamentally the same. So we need not be concerned about reaching a particular level or state of serenity. That will take care of itself in time. The aim of practice is just to practice. It's good at the beginning, and it's good at the end. Zazen is zazen.

I would like to sit every day, but I have a job and a family so I am usually busy from morning till night. I can't seem to find time to practice regularly.

We all have our particular problems, our particular situations in life. So we have to find solutions to suit those particular conditions. I think that if we have a sincere desire to practice zazen, we can usually find a way to do so.

If we are too busy to practice every day, is there anything we can do in our daily lives which will have the same effect as zazen? For example, should we try to sit with a straight back when we are working?

Of course it's nice to maintain good posture in all our activities, but if we worry about the condition of our spines while we are cutting vegetables, we might cut our fingers instead. Just to do whatever you are doing, wholeheartedly, is a kind of practice, a kind of zazen. But to learn to do that is very difficult. That is why we need to practice zazen. There is really no substitute for zazen itself.

But if it is really too difficult...

The situation is quite simple, really. If it is difficult, you should practice. If it is impossible, you can't!

I find it difficult to understand the relation between zazen and everyday life. If we must practice in order to enter the state of natural balance, it seems that we must practice continuously in order to maintain that state. Doesn't the state in zazen disappear as soon as we finish the practice?

No, it continues for some time.

Why?

Because the state in zazen is not an artificial state which we manufacture through our efforts on the zazen cushion. It is, as I have said many times, our natural state, or our original state. So when we come back to our original state in zazen, it will stay with us for some time after the practice is over. It

will cling to us or follow us naturally. Master Dogen compared
it to the ringing of a bell. When we strike a bell, the sound
continues for a long time. When we practice zazen every day, it
is like striking a bell in a slow, steady rhythm. The vibra-
tions of the first practice carry through to the next, and we
can thus live continuously in the state of natural balance.

*My problem is that I sometimes get very sleepy while practicing
zazen. What should I do?*

You should wake up!

*Perhaps my problem is the same, but I don't feel sleepy in
zazen. I just feel bored. I really find it very monotonous to
sit still for forty-five minutes, staring at a wall. It is very
hard for me to deal with that boredom.*

The problem of boredom is very interesting. This modern world
of ours esteems excitement very much. People are always seeking
intensity, drama, and interest. We look for excitement in the
realms of thought and physical pleasure, and we become restless
in situations which provide no special stimulation, no intellectual or sensory kick. This is our orientation, our habitual
attitude or point of view. So when we first experience zazen,
it is natural to find it boring. Perhaps, for a while, we can
entertain ourselves with thoughts or mental fantasies, and
after that the problem of our painful legs and backs may absorb
our attention, but sooner or later, we are likely to encounter
a sense of boredom. I think that encounter with boredom may be
very important, for, in a sense, life itself is boring.

Gautama Buddha taught us that life is action. It is one action,
after another, after another. It is getting up, washing our
faces, and eating breakfast. It is eating, sleeping, and washing our clothes. There is no excitement in such activities.
They are very simple, very repetitive and monotonous. It seems
tedious to do the same things, day after day, year after year,
but, tedious or not, such activities are the fundamental basis

of life. This is the Buddhist understanding, the Buddhist viewpoint or orientation. Buddhism states that life is eating,
sleeping, and washing clothes. Eating, sleeping, and washing
clothes are the essence of life in the real world.

So if we are to know the real world, we must see it as it is.
We must learn to appreciate the simple and monotonous activities which are the real basis of our lives, our culture, and
our civilization. Such an outlook is contrary to our usual way
of thinking. To attain such an outlook, we need a kind of revolution in our bodies and minds. Such a revolution can occur
only through the practice of zazen. Zazen can teach us the
value of seemingly boring activities. Zazen can teach us to
appreciate and enjoy the simple activites which are the basis
of life. When we practice zazen, we can transcend boredom and
excitement. At first, we may cling to our habitual patterns of
thought—we may seek excitement even in the simple act of sitting—but after some time, we will forget excitement and boredom altogether. Then we will discover that zazen is not a
boring activity, but life itself. In that simple discovery, we
can find the true meaning of life. We can find what to do and
what not to do, very clearly. We can do what needs to be done
and avoid doing what should not be done. We can begin a new
life—a life of Buddhist action.

So if you find zazen boring, it is possible that you are touching the heart of Buddhism itself. Don't run away from it. Meet
it directly. Become friends with boredom. Enjoy boredom. If you
can find the value of boredom, you will find the value of
zazen. Then your whole life will be changed.

*The revolution you speak of—would we necessarily be aware that
it had occurred?*

We need not recognize the revolution. To be practicing zazen is
the revolution itself. To practice zazen is to believe in
zazen. To practice zazen is the evidence that the revolution
has already occurred. But it is not a one-shot deal. We must

continue to practice zazen every day. Continuing our practice
every day is the maintenance of the revolution in our bodies
and minds. It is the evidence that we are living in the new
world—the world of Buddhist action.

*You say that to practice zazen is to believe in zazen. Is it
necessary to believe in Buddhism in order to practice zazen?
Can we simply practice zazen and not become involved in believ-
ing?*

Usually we think that belief is a matter of intellect, a matter
thinking. But I think belief is more than a matter of what we
think. It is also a question of what we do. It is intimately
connected with our action. Therefore, to practice zazen is to
believe in zazen already. If you want to practice zazen, you
are a Buddhist already. If you don't want to practice zazen,
you are not a Buddhist yet. Our actions and our conduct teach
us what we really believe.

THE FOUR PHILOSOPHIES

I think we have just about reached the end of our story. We have traced Buddhist theory from the ideal of the Middle Way, through the materialistic schema of the twelve-fold chain of cause and effect, and finally to the theory of action and the idea of an instantaneous reality. At that point we learned that theory is not enough. If we want to meet real Buddhism, we must transcend theory, and to transcend theory we must really act: we must practice zazen. To practice zazen is to meet real Buddhism. It is to meet the Real Dragon, face to face.

So it seems that we have come to a very natural stopping point in our study of Buddhist theory. Zazen is ALL of Buddhism. There is nothing more to do or say—or is there? In fact there is much to do and much to say. There are many ideas, theories, and problems which remain to be discussed, explored, and dealt with in much greater depth than is possible in the pages of this book. A mature and thorough understanding of Buddhism requires many years of study and practice, and much practical experience of real life. My original aim in writing this book was to provide a kind of foundation on which such a mature understanding might grow and evolve. I wanted to present the fundamental ideas of Buddhism in such a way that the internal logic of Buddhist philosophy would be revealed, for it is my belief that if the people of the modern world could learn the

Buddhist system of thought, they would find new insights into the roots of their personal confusion and new methods of understanding and resolving the conflicts at the heart of human civilization.

This logical system of Buddhist thought is, of course, the four philosophies. Even before I studied Buddhism, I had gained some intuitive understanding of the fundamental attitudes and viewpoints of human beings. This understanding had come directly from my own experience. But it was only after I encountered the works of Master Dogen that the real logic of life began to be clear. It seems appropriate, therefore, to conclude this book with a short discussion of the opening lines of that king of all Buddhist books: the *Shōbōgenzō*.

There are several editions of the *Shōbōgenzō* in existence today. Among them there are some differences in the number and arrangement of chapters. The oldest edition has seventy-five chapters, the first titled "Genjo Koan" or "The Real Universe." It is the opening lines of that chapter that I would like to quote here. I believe that they are a kind of key to the Buddhist logic which Master Dogen employs throughout the *Shōbōgenzō*.

> When the universe is seen from the standpoint which regards all things as meaningful teachings of Buddhism, there is delusion and enlightenment, Buddhist practice, life and death, Buddhas and ordinary people. When the universe is considered objectively, there is no delusion and no enlightenment, no Buddhas and no ordinary people, no life and no death. Buddhism is originally transcendent over relativism, over abundance and scarcity. Even so, there is life and death, delusion and enlightenment, ordinary people and Buddhas. The reality is that flowers fall even though we love them, and weeds grow even though we hate them.

The first sentence in this series explains the universe as seen

from the standpoint of the subject or the self. When there is a
subject, all things are seen in relation to that subject, and
all things have meaning in relation to that subject. Some
things are seen as good, others as bad. Some things are seen as
having value, others are seen as valueless, or as having negative value in relation to the subject. Thus, at this phase,
there is delusion which is bad and enlightenment which is good.
There is life which is valuable and death which is the absence
of value. There are Buddhas who are great and ordinary people
who are just ordinary people. This is, in other words, the
standpoint of idealism. The idealist is, above all, concerned
with value, with meaning, with ideas and concepts which enable
him to understand and evaluate the world as he encounters it.
The relativistic nature of life as seen from the idealistic
standpoint is very clear.

In the next sentence, we find a standpoint which appears to
reject relativism. This is the standpoint without the self or
the subject. It is the standpoint of utter objectivism or
materialism. When the universe is seen from this standpoint,
there can be no question of meaning or value in relation to the
subject because the existence of the subject is denied. Without
the self, there can be no differences in value. Nothing can
have meaning beyond the simple fact of its existence. Thus,
from this standpoint, there is only matter or form. There is no
enlightenment as opposed to delusion, no Buddhas as opposed to
ordinary people. There is no absolute difference between life
and death itself. All such things are only concepts; they have
no real existence in the world.

The materialistic viewpoint, thus, at first appears to be the
viewpoint of stark realism. It appears to transcend the rela-
tivity of idealism, but in fact it does not, for the existence
of the world of matter depends upon the existence of a per-
ceiver. Without a subject to receive sensory impressions from
the external world, the external world could not exist. So the
materialistic viewpoint is also a kind of relativism, a viewpoint which implicitly acknowledges the division between the

subject and the object. The relativism of the idealist is based on the division between the subject which thinks and the objects of his thought. The relativism of the materialist is based on the division between the subject which feels or senses and the objects of his perception. The fundamental difference between the two viewpoints is thus simply a matter of where the weight of attention is placed. In the case of the idealist, the focus of attention is the interior world of the mind or the spirit, while in the case of the materialist, all attention is focused on the world outside: the external world of matter or form.

In the third sentence, Master Dogen expresses the realistic Buddhist attitude toward life. He states that Buddhism completely transcends relativistic viewpoints. A Buddhist does not discriminate between this and that on the basis of idealistic concepts of value or materialistic denials of value and meaning. He thus transcends both abundance and scarcity. Freed of such discriminations, he finds the real world as it is. Thus, there is the appearance and disappearance of real things in the world. There is real life and real death, real Buddhas and real ordinary people. They just exist, as they are. This is the Buddhist understanding, the Buddhist philosophy of reality.

But a philosophy of reality is not reality itself. We cannot presume to know reality simply by speaking of the transcendence of abundance and scarcity, or affirming the existence of all things as they are. Reality is something beyond theory, whether that theory happens to be idealistic, materialistic, or Buddhistic in nature. Thus, Master Dogen could only point toward that reality which is beyond theory. This is the meaning of the last sentence in the series. Here, falling flowers and weeds are symbols of the ineffable reality itself. The reality is that flowers fall even though we love them and weeds grow even though we hate them. We cannot really understand this world precisely. It has a sacred quality, an ineffable quality that defies all our efforts to grasp, understand or change. It is just there, like falling flowers and stubborn weeds. It just exists, as it is, whether we like it or not.

QUESTIONS & ANSWERS

Does the line about falling flowers and growing weeds mean that reality includes and transcends human emotions, or that our emotional reactions are somehow irrelevant to what actually exists?

I think the latter understanding is better. In this sentence Master Dogen is talking about seeing the world as it is. He is talking about recognizing the raw and simple face of existing reality. Flowers fall. Weeds grow. We need not feel any joy or sorrow. This is just the way things are. This is the Truth.

Master Dogen's words seem rather cold and impersonal. It is difficult for me to see the connection between his intellectual explanations and the practical problems of my life.

Yes, Master Dogen's explanation here is very philosophical, very precise and analytical. But I think we need such explanations. We need such explanations because without them it is very difficult to learn the true meaning of Buddhism and the Buddhist attitude toward life. By studying Master Dogen's words we can gradually understand his outlook and his way of thinking; in time we can attain our own Buddhist attitude. And when we have attained our own Buddhist attitude, these somewhat dry and theoretical sentences will come to have a very direct and personal meaning in our real lives.

That may be true—in the future—but for now I find your practical explanations much more helpful and satisfying. I wonder if you could once again explain how the four philosophies develop in the natural course of our lives?

When we are young it is very natural to dream. We have many ideas and many aims. We yearn to achieve those aims, to realize those dreams. To have many dreams and idealistic thoughts about life is rather romantic and beautiful, but when those ideas absorb our attention, it becomes very difficult to recognize the real world in which we are living. We cannot see the wall that divides the real world from the world of ideas and dreams. And so we run into that wall again and again. We bump our heads and bloody our noses time after time in our efforts to reach the aims which exist only in our minds. And so Buddhism counsels us to beware of the illusory nature of ideas and dreams. Budhism urges us to adopt a critical attitude toward idealistic thinking. This means that at times we must forget our dreams. At times we must coldly reject our romantic ideas about life.

When we reject the idealistic attitude toward life, we have a tendency to fall into a kind of materialistic hell. We lose our ideals. We scorn sincere effort as a waste of time. We indulge in physical pleasures of all kinds, and we lose the dreams which make our lives vivid and vigorous. This is clearly not a happy alternative to an idealistic life. We should not become animals. We should endeavor to maintain our dignity as human beings. But at the same time we should not be romantic dreamers who never see the simplest facts of life. Therefore, at the second stage, we should study those facts of life. We should look at the external world objectively and study it scientifically. This is an important task and an important phase in our understanding. Through the scientific study of life we can begin to move toward a realistic involvement in the real world.

Such an involvement is the focus of the third stage. Here we should find the world of action. We should study what action is through action itself. Entering the world of action is a new and sometimes frightening experience for a person who has lived most of his life in the realms of thought and sensation. In the world of action we lose the tried and trusted ideas on which our former lives were based. Life suddenly becomes very sharp and uncertain. It is momentary, vivid, and dangerous. It is REAL. In such a world our actions must inevitably be sincere, but unfortunately, they will not always be correct. We make many mistakes. We blunder again and again. But we cannot give up. We cannot retreat. We must continue our very severe and serious, sometimes bloody and dangerous life of action on the basis of intuition and the painfully accumulated knowldege of trial and error.

Finally we must acknowledge the need for some kind of guide or standard. We want to continue our vibrant lives in the world of action, but we are tired of being knocked about. We want to eliminate some of our mistakes and enjoy a bit of peace and quiet. We want to set a reasonably straight course and maintain it for awhile without constant checking and the fear that we will go wrong. But where can we find such a guide? Where can we find such a standard? For thousands of years we have searched the horizons for the ultimate guide, the ultimate purpose, the ultimate Truth. We have looked in countless distant places for the true aim of life. Guatama Buddha advised us to change the focus of our search. He advised us to look for the ultimate aim of life, not on the horizons of the universe, but in the center of ourselves. He advised us to practice zazen. When we practice zazen we can find the guide. We can find the standard. We can find the aim, and we can find ourselves. And when we find ourselves in zazen, we will discover that the aim and the self are one and the same.

THE DRAGON HAS MANY FACES

To study Buddhism is not so easy. Buddhist philosophy is very broad, very deep, and very subtle. It has many standpoints, many contradictory modes of thinking about life and the world. In the chapters of this book we have looked at those standpoints one by one. We have considered many problems from many sides. In doing so, we have had just a taste of what it means to study Buddhist philosophy. I hope that taste has whetted your appetite. I hope you feel some urge to dig deeper, some desire to find the Real Dragon in your life. If so, I hope you will remember that Buddhist philosophy is but one face of the Dragon. It is an interesting face, an intriguing face, a face which can absorb our attention and become an important reference point in our day-to-day lives. I have been studying Buddhist thought, as explained by Master Dogen, for over forty years. In that time, it has never become stale or boring. To me, Master Dogen's words are always fresh and alive. They always teach me something about my life, here and now. But even the words of Master Dogen cannot teach us everything about life. No matter how interesting philosophical thought may be, we must, at some point, acknowledge its limits. Sooner or later we have to raise our heads from our books and look around us. Sooner or later we have to look at the real situation in the world. The real situation in the world is the second face of the Dragon.

Studying the real situation in the world is not a comforting or encouraging exercise. Everywhere we look we find problems. At the individual level there is the problem of health and sanity, the problem of maintaining our physical and mental equilibrium in the midst of a chaotic world. Our relations with that world are always problematic. Conflicts between people arise at every level of society. Children fight with their parents. Lovers quarrel. Husbands and wives sue for divorce. Communities and nations pursue their own limited interests without regard for the needs and aspirations of others on the globe. It is all very discouraging. We are tempted to close our eyes, to return to the safety and security of our philosophy books. But that won't do. That really won't do. We must press on with our study. We must try to see and understand the world as it actually exists.

I think the world is understandable. I think there are clear patterns in the seemingly chaotic relations among men and nations. It may be dangerous and simplistic to generalize, but I think it is important to do so, for without some effort to reduce or simplify the great mass of information confronting us, it is very difficult to make sense of anything in this complicated world. Thus, when I look at the broad patterns of political, social, and economic activity on the globe today, the existence of two conflicting groups of nations is impossible to ignore.

The conflicting groups of nations are closely identified with two very powerful countries: the United States and the Soviet Union. Those nations and peoples which look, however grudgingly or reluctantly, to the United States for leadership, example, or simple protection, generally see themselves as the defenders of individual freedom and other liberalistic values. Those in the Soviet sphere of influence tend to regard themselves as participants in a revolutionary movement. They are riding the crest of an evolutionary wave—a wave of political, economic, and social forces which is moving inexorably toward a utopian society of perfect equality and harmony.

THE DRAGON HAS MANY FACES

Such self-perceptions reveal the underlying source of tension
between these two groups of countries, that is, the conflicting
philosophies or world-views on which they are based. The leaders of the liberalistic countries of the West are struggling to
maintain the idealistic beliefs on which their countries were
established. The principle sources of those beliefs are the
Western religions, especially Christianity. Christianity, as
most will acknowledge, is becoming weaker and weaker as the
advances of natural science progressively diminish the sphere
over which spiritual thought may rule. It is thus becoming more
and more difficult for the people of liberalistic societies to
find support for their beliefs. Many have in fact abandoned
the world-views of their ancestors and have adopted more-or-
less materialistic outlooks toward life. The Western countries
have thus become uneasy amalgams of contradictory beliefs and
policies; their leaders often appear two-faced and irrational
as they pursue materialistic power while espousing the traditional beliefs of idealistic religions.

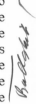

By comparison, the leaders of the Societ bloc nations often
seem more consistent and rational in their policies and views.
They are, atleast on the surface, untroubled by the conflict
between traditional religious beliefs and modern materialistic
explanations. They can welcome every new advance of science as
a confirmation of their own beliefs, for their countries were
established on the basis of Marxism, and Marxism is a materialistic philosophy. It believes in no god. It believes in no
"religious" ideas. It insists that the universe is only matter
and energy.

The people in the liberalistic countries cannot accept this
theory. In spite of (or because of) their present confusion
about the real nature of life, they want to believe in something other than matter. They want to believe in the reality of
thought and the truth of their ideals. They intuitively understand that materialistic thought has no room for such beliefs,
and so they perceive the Marxist countries as a very real
threat to their identity and to the very survival of spiritual

221   SEEKING THE TRUTH IN A WORLD OF CHAOS   221

or idealistic thought.

This is, I believe, the fundamental cause of tension on the globe today. I believe that the philosophical conflict between idealism and materialism has found its physical form in the two groups of countries which have emerged and defined themselves in the modern world. So we can say that the conflict between the two groups of countries in the world is a conflict between two religions or two beliefs, and when we consider this fact we must also be aware of a very queer tendency of human beings, that is, their tendency to fight and die for what they believe. Men have demonstrated this peculiar tendency again and again in the history of the world. Wherever and whenever societies with conflicting beliefs have encountered one another, the resolution of the conflict has come only through the severe test of war. In those wars many men have died. They have died for their beliefs. It is a very sad fact, a very miserable tendency, but one we dare not ignore—for the next war cannot be just another war. The next war could be the final war, the final event in the history of human beings. This is the terrible power which mankind has produced. It has found the power to destroy itself and the entire world.

I think people are well aware of the danger of nuclear war. For many, the possibility of nuclear war is just too terrible to consider. It is unthinkable, and yet, as we see the nuclear stockpiles grow and the missiles increase in number day by day, we know in our hearts that the unthinkable has somehow become a real possibility in the world. People have always recognized the danger of war, but this has not stopped them from fighting for what they believe. Danger, by itself, is not a sufficient deterrent to war. The only way to remove the possibility of war is to solve the conflict itself, and when I consider this very grave necessity, I cannot help thinking that Buddhism could provide the basis for such a solution.

Buddhism has its four-phased system of thought. In the first two phases it acknowledges the positive aspects of idealistic and materialistic thought, while recognizing the dangers and limitations of both viewpoints. It then provides an alternative to these extreme philosophies by suggesting a new way of looking at life and the universe. The philosophy of action teaches us about the unity of all things at the moment of the present. It urges us to consider the meaning of real time and real existence. By focusing our attention on the here and now it forces us to look at our lives from a new and unfamiliar standpoint. It gives us a new sense of priorities, a new outlook or attitude which can help us to resolve the conflicts between our spiritual and materialistic tendencies. Finally, Buddhism provides a method of experiencing the unity which the philosophy of action proclaims. Zazen unifies the spiritual world and the material world. In zazen, the worlds of thinking and feeling are combined into oneness. All things are part of that oneness. Nothing is excluded. Nothing is denied. Is it too optimistic then to hope that Buddhism might show us the way to avoid the final war?

If liberalistic countries found that there was a religion in the world which affirmed the fundamental dignity of human beings without resorting to theories of spiritual realms apart from this world; and if, at the same time, Marxist countries studied Buddhism and discovered thereby that there was a very rational basis for belief in something other than matter; then, would there not be some ground for compromise between the two groups of countries? If liberalistic and Marxist countries both studied the theories of Buddhism would they not find the existence of a religion which affirms the real world: a world which includes the spiritual and materialistic sides of life. And if they believed in this theory, would they not find that they in fact believed in the same religion, the one true religion of human beings?

Is my idea too optimistic?—too fantastic? Yes, I think so. The world is moving too fast. Events beyond our control are increasing tension in the world, day by day. To believe that Buddhism could spread through the world in time to save us from destruction is a kind of dream, I suppose. It is a dream which can exist only in my brain. It is very regrettable to me, but it is true, I'm afraid. And other people who believe in Buddhism can also dream of a peaceful Buddhist world, and their dreams, like mine, will exist only in their brains. But if such people increased in number throughout the globe, might not the situation itself be changed? Perhaps. Perhaps not. We cannot forsee what the future will bring. It is very difficult to be optimistic, but I think we need not give up hope. We can have hope. We can make our efforts in this life. We can look clearly at the miserable situations in the world and still have hope, because, as human beings, we always have perfect freedom to try. We always have perfect freedom to make our efforts for a better life and a better world. So our real situation is very miserable and discouraging, but at the same time, very bright and hopeful. This is the real nature of life according to Buddhism. To do our best in every situation is to express our true nature as human beings. The end result is not so important. To do our best is our best.

But how can we do our best? What does it mean, to do our best? Isn't it too vague?—too wishy-washy? In a sense it is. We cannot really try to save the world. Our real problems, here and now, are not problems of global tension, or the conflicts between various countries. Our lives, here and now, have a very simple, primitive quality, and our real problems share that very basic and primitive character. They are simple, everyday problems. Problems like making money to buy food and pay the rent. Problems of finding time to do the grocery shopping. Problems of choosing which vegetables to buy and which not to buy. Our lives are full of such problems. The problems demand decisions, right now. They demand action at the moment of the present. We must decide how many potatoes to peel for dinner and which pot to boil them in. We must peel the potatoes, one by one. We must cut them up and put them in the pot with the right amount of water.

The attention we give to such tasks is very important. Such

tasks are the substance of our lives. If we perform such tasks
well, our lives will take on a sense of harmony and balance. If
our attention wavers, we are likely to make a mess. We are
likely to lose our balance at any moment and at every monent.
So living well requires some simple, direct effort from moment
to moment. It requires a certain sincerity. The sincerity, for
example, or a child tying his shoes for the first time. This is
the real meaning of doing our best. It is the real meaning of
life. When we do all things with a sense of care and total *What?*
involvement, there can be no real problems in our lives. Our
lives and the world itself assume a simple and straightforward
appearance. This is the true face of the world, here and now.
It is the third face of the Dragon.

And what of the fourth face of the Dragon? What can be said of
the final Truth, the ultimate reality of zazen? Many words
might be spoken. Many words have in fact been said. Poets of
all ages have attempted to capture the ineffable in words. If
I were a poet, I would tell you of fleeting images, of simple
sensations in the here and now. I would speak of momentary
sights and sounds coming and going in the stillness, in the
quietness. Yes, if I were a poet, I would tell you of the music
of the silence. I would tell you of the beauty of sitting in
quietness. But I am not a poet. I am a simple man in a complex
world. And so I ony know that zazen is zazen.

These are the words of Master Dogen. He was a true poet. He
spoke of the state in zazen with many beautiful words. He said
that zazen was a state like the sea. The sea, like man himself,
is a unity of two worlds. The surface of the sea is like the
mind. At times it is dark and stormy—full of violent waves and
chaotic movement. At other times it is clear, bright, and calm,
like a mirror or a mountain lake on a peaceful summer day.
These are only the passing moods of the sea. They exist only on
the surface of the water.

At the bottom of the sea, there is perpetual darkness, stillness and peace. Here there are no storms or violence. The great

body of the sea is unperturbed by the fluctuating moods of the surface world. In this it is like the human body when it assumes the posture of zazen. To take our seats on the round, black cushions, fold our legs, and straighten our backs, is to settle into the state of original peace and contentment. When we take the posture of zazen, day after day, our bodies learn their standard condition. They welcome the chance to return to the silent state, to the deep calm of the sea. When we have found this state, nothing can disturb our sense of inner harmony and repose. The stormy moods of the mind simply cannot persist for long. To balance the body is to balance the mind. To practice zazen is to enter the state which always exists beneath the fleeting surface storms. It is to enter the state like the sea.

But images of the sea are only images. Words are only words. They can suggest the real, but they cannot capture the real itself. In the end, Master Dogen himself could say nothing of the ineffable state in zazen. So finally he said what must be said: zazen is just zazen. In the end, all things are just as they are. This is the ultimate Truth, the final conclusion. Many people suppose that zazen is a way to attain the Truth, but such people are deluded by misty images of the Dragon. To practice zazen is to meet the Real Dragon. It is to become the Dragon itself. Thus, zazen is the Truth itself. It is Buddhism itself. Zazen is Zazen.

Its whole body—a voice
hanging in space.
The wind bell doesn't worry
about the wind's direction,
north, south, east, or west
always it preaches real wisdom:
Chin, tin, ton, rin,
Chin, tin, ton.